BELIEVE THE GOOD NEWS

BELIEVE THE GOOD NEWS

DAILY MEDITATIONS ON THE LENTEN MASSES

EMERIC LAWRENCE O.S.B.

THE LITURGICAL PRESS
COLLEGEVILLE, MINNESOTA

Cover by Sr. Mary Charles McGough, O.S.B.

Nihil obstat: Robert C. Harren, J.C.L., *Censor deputatus.*
Imprimatur: ✛George H. Speltz, D.D., Bishop of St. Cloud. January 12, 1982.

Library of Congress Cataloging in Publication Data

Lawrence, Emeric Anthony, 1908–
    Believe the good news.

    1. Lent — Meditations.   I. Title.
BX2170.L4L38   242'.34   82-97
ISBN 0-8146-1256-3   AACR2

CONTENTS

INSIGHTS INTO LENT

Every thoughtful Christian instinctively recognizes that Lent is a very special, grace-filled, and challenging time of the year. This is one reason why many of us have probably experienced certain sentiments of dissatisfaction with past Lents. We instinctively sense that "we ought to have gotten more out of it," that it ought to have meant more to us than it did.

Many have also probably noticed a development in the meaning of Lent in recent years. For older Catholics much of the emphasis was on fasting and abstaining from certain foods, from alcohol and smoking, movies, etc., along with some added spiritual exercises like daily Mass and/or spiritual reading. It was mainly an exercise in self-discipline that was hopefully related to the Passion of our Lord, but for the most part we hardly saw it as being related to the yearly renewal of the entire Church. Nor did we place much emphasis on the personal renewal of our baptism or on personal conversion to Christ. Conversion, we thought, was for Protestants who had decided to become Catholics and were taking instructions in Catholic doctrine. But now more and more we see personal conversion for ourselves as an ongoing, life-long process of turning to Christ and allowing him to take over the direction of our lives. It is a life-long process of being filled with the ideals of the Gospel of Jesus. It is growing up in Christ. And it is not only for individual Christians, but for the entire Church.

But there is something else. On Tuesday of the first week of Lent we will pray: "Father, look on us, your children. Through the discipline of Lent *help us to grow in our desire for you.*" What greater favor can we request than a deeper desire for God? St. Augustine remarked long ago about our restless, desire-filled hearts. He told us that the only one who could satisfy those hungry hearts was God himself. But the fulfillment comes only in proportion to the depth and genuineness of our desire. Hence our prayer — and hence one of the chief purposes of Lent: "Help us to grow in our desire for you." The more spiritually restless we are and the greater our hunger and desire for God, the greater will be our satisfaction at

Easter this year and ultimately at the greatest Easter of all, the moment of our passover from life in this world to him who alone can finally and completely satisfy us.

The purpose of this book might well be summed up as an attempt to make the desire for God more available to the thoughtful Christian. Each of the Lenten Masses is a call from God to us to come back to him and be filled with his being, his love, his truth. This book is intended to help us to respond to the call with ready, eager hearts and minds. I have reflected on the meaning, not only of the Word of God in the readings and the psalms but also the prayers. I have sought, not always successfully to be sure, to discern a main theme that will stand out and remain with the reader through the day and longer. As a special aid towards lodging the main idea of the Mass in our minds, several verses from psalms, readings, or prayers of the Mass are added at the end of the reflection. I suggest that the reader memorize one or the other of these texts and repeat them frequently during the day. The memorizing and care-filled repetition can in itself become an enduring prayer.

But I hope that the thoughtful, loving reading of each meditation will also become prayer. It would be useful, of course, to have the entire Mass text available as part of the meditation, but the old daily missals are no longer available (except for the *New St. Joseph Daily Missal* and the *New St. Joseph Sunday Missal* — published by the Catholic Book Publishing Co., New York City). However, most parishes provide missalettes for the people which — while they do not contain the entire text of the readings — do at least give the texts of the various Mass antiphons and the Responsorial Psalm, with Scripture references to the entire text.

This set of insights into the meaning of Lent would be incomplete without mention of its great potential for helping us to acquire a deeper appreciation and understanding of the three central sacraments of our faith — baptism, the Eucharist, the sacrament of reconciliation (Penance).

Too long has baptism been understood as a merely negative "washing away of the stain of original sin" in the person to be baptized. There was little consideration of baptism as a triumphant rebirth into the redeemed community of God's holy people, the Church. Most of us were baptized as infants. The Masses of Lent help us to realize the greatness and blessedness of this rebirth and to look forward to our personal ratification of that rebirth during the Easter Vigil when as mature Christians we renew our baptismal commitment to Christ and his Church.

Lent also brings us face-to-face with our sinful human condition.

It makes us realize that sin is not just a personal fault that deprives us of grace but rather that it alienates us from God and from the community of the redeemed. Jesus gave us a special sacrament — reconciliation — whose principal aims are to reconcile us with God and the people of God, whose corporate health we have diminished by our sins, and to restore us to full and profitable membership.

Lent is a favored time for restoring this sacrament to its rightful and necessary position in our spiritual life — the living out of our baptism. Each confession can be all of Lent in miniature. It is concerned with conversion, rebirth, restoration, reconciliation. It sharpens our desire for God, and it builds us up and provides spiritual strength against further falls from grace and from the community.

Finally, Lent brings us to a deeper appreciation and love for the greatest treasure we have as Christians — the Blessed Eucharist, the Mass. If confession is "Lent in miniature," the Mass is more: It actually makes the entire redeeming life, work, and sacrifice of Jesus present on our altars. It is hard for us to grasp the full implications of this reality, which is another reason why we need Lent so badly. Day by day Lent leads us along a road of ever-growing appreciation of the historical life, death, and resurrection of Jesus, now made present on our altars, so that we can take it to ourselves and add our own loving sacrificial life to it.

If this book helps readers to grow in their desire for God and in a deeper appreciation of their heritage as members of the redeemed people of God, I will feel deeply blessed. "Hear, O Lord, the sound of my call . . . of you my heart speaks; you my glance seeks. Your presence, O Lord, I seek. Hide not your face from me" (Responsorial Psalm, Second Sunday of Lent).

ACKNOWLEDGEMENTS

These meditations were first tried out on two of my friends, Fr. Angelo Zankl, O.S.B., my fellow chaplain at St. Scholastica Priory, and Sr. Timothy Kirby, O.S.B., assistant student chaplain and counselor at the College of St. Scholastica. I am grateful to them for their approval and suggestions for improving the work. I am also most grateful to LeMay Bechtold and Fr. Daniel Durken, O.S.B., for their pertinent and valuable suggestions, to Sr. Mary Charles McGough, O.S.B., for designing the cover, and to the editors of The Liturgical Press for preparing the manuscript for publishing.

Fr. Emeric A. Lawrence, O.S.B.
St. Scholastica Priory
Duluth, Minnesota

READING I　Joel 2:12-18　　　　　　READING II　2 Cor 5:20-6:2
GOSPEL　　Matt 6:1-6, 16-18

Reading I:　The prophet Joel outlines a positive program for a sincere and honest return to God for those who have forsaken him: "Return to me with your whole heart . . . ."

Reading II:　"Now is the acceptable time! Now is the day of salvation." This is a perfect description of what Lent can and ought to be for each and all Christians — and the Church as well.

Gospel:　Jesus lists the traditional Lenten practices — prayer, fasting, almsgiving — and he insists that these can benefit us only if motivated by love of God rather than the desire for reward or any kind of human acclaim.

"Remember, man, that you are dust, and to dust you shall return!" Such was the traditional Ash Wednesday greeting that Mother Church used to give her children. The words took on dramatic meaning when the priest traced a cross made of ashes on the forehead of the Christian. The words were used for the first time when, according to Genesis 3:19, Adam and Eve refused to remember their origin as creatures, wanted to be like unto God, the Creator, and so introduced sin and evil into creation. As we recall from our Bible history, their eyes were opened not only to the disturbing fact of their nakedness but to the dramatic and awful sense of having rejected love, having cut themselves off from divine friendship, and having found themselves all alone with their creatureliness.

God did promise them some distant and mysterious salvation (Gen 3:15), but after outlining the kind of life they and their descendants would have to expect, he reminded them of their origins in the dust of the earth: "You are dust and to dust you shall return."

All sin is rebellion against God; it is refusal to remember our creatureliness, whether it be the sin of our first parents or the pre-Lenten carousings and revels that characterize carnival time in so many Catholic countries. The idea of carnival seemed to be to sin enthusiastically, even wildly; then receive the ashes and determine to "make up for" our sins by doing penance for a few weeks, and then all will be well again. Just so we remember: "You are dust and to dust you shall return."

One can question whether this heavy emphasis on sin contained in the traditional formula for the imposition of ashes is what Lent is mainly about. I for one prefer the positive invitation to growth contained in the alternate formula now permitted by the Church:

"Turn away from sin and be faithful to the gospel." Note how the very opening verse of the Ash Wednesday liturgy sets the theme and tone of Lent as it should be regarded: "Lord, you are merciful to all, and hate nothing you have created. You overlook the sins of men to bring them to repentance. You are the Lord our God" (Entrance Antiphon).

Self-hatred or self-disgust may well be a natural human reaction to sins of weakness we Christians are guilty of. There are some who actually cultivate this self-disgust to the point of wallowing in guilt. It is not a healthy, and surely not a Christian, reaction. It contradicts the inspired words already quoted. The Lord is merciful to all, no matter what they have done. He hates nothing he has created, and surely he does not want those he has created — frail, vulnerable human beings that we are — to hate ourselves.

The one thing God does hate is sin, not for what it does to him, but for what it does to us whom he loves. It diminishes us as persons, retards our growth in friendship with him, and frustrates our hunger for true joy and happiness. So he "overlooks" our sins (an expressive term for "forgives") in order *to bring us to repentance*, to a new wholeness. Fr. John Shea in *The Challenge of Jesus* gives a perfect description of the ideal kind of repentance we can aim at during Lent: "Jesus does not convict the world of sin by emphasizing its guilt *but by being grace to it*" (Chicago: Thomas More Press, 1975, 60, emphasis added).

The Church is realistic, as is God himself. She takes into account that her children are weak, "fallen," constantly inclined to evil and in danger of falling again and again. Like God himself, the Church during Lent is concerned with repentance in her members, a change of mind and heart. But she wants change to be motivated, not by self-hatred arising from a sense of self-defeat, nor by self-exaltation arising from successful self-discipline through fasting and other penitential acts, but by an awareness of the goodness and lovableness of God. Who could improve on the way the prophet Joel lays out the objective of Lent?

> Even now, says the Lord, return to me with your whole heart,
> with fasting, and weeping, and mourning;
> rend your hearts, not your garments,
> and return to the Lord, your God.
> For gracious and merciful is he . . . (Reading I).

Christians have to know themselves if they are to be proper prospects for becoming the Lord's new creations during this Lent. They have to be aware of their weaknesses and moral defects and their causes. But they are not to be defeatists, just as they are not to be self-despisers. Like the psalmist they can say, "I acknowledge my offense, and my sin is before me always." But they also recognize that sin is not letting themselves down; it is letting God down. "Against you only have I sinned, and done what is evil in your sight."

Most important of all, at this beginning of Lent, Christians understand that the Lord again calls them to a new beginning, a new creation. He never gives up on us. "A clean heart create for me, O Lord, and a steadfast spirit renew within me. . . . Give me back the joy of your salvation, and a willing spirit sustain in me."

Just as Christian morality is not the result of the observing of laws and rules (that's what we call "ethics"), but rather responsiveness to a Person, Christ, so the conversion to which Christ summons us today and always (the call never weakens) takes its rise from our recognition of Jesus as love in person. Fr. Adrian Nocent, O.S.B., puts it perfectly: "The Church refuses to make sin the center of religion. The focus of Christianity is not on sin but on Christ who conquered sin and death" (*The Liturgical Year*, vol. 2 [Lent], Collegeville, Minn.: The Liturgical Press, 1977, 11).

"The Church refuses to make sin the focus of Christianity. . . ." That may come as a surprise to many Catholics and other Christians, but it's the truth that emerges inevitably out of the Scriptures and above all the Gospels. Plainly put, the best possible program for the Christian during Lent would be to come to know Jesus more and more intimately by reading and meditating on the Gospels. It is he who creates new and clean hearts within us, but he cannot do it unless we know from him why we need and desire new hearts. This may well be what the Church has in mind in today's Communion Antiphon: "The person who meditates day and night on the law of the Lord will yield fruit in due season." It is not impossible or unreasonable or doing violence to the meaning of Scripture to change "law of the Lord" to "Jesus, Son of God," and then we have a perfect Lenten program.

* * *

"Be merciful, O Lord, for we have sinned" (*Responsorial Psalm*).

"If today you hear his voice, harden not your hearts" (*Gospel Verse*).

"Even now, says the Lord, return to me with your whole heart" (*Reading I*).

As a means for recalling the content of each daily meditation, I suggest that the reader *memorize* one of these texts and repeat it often during the day. This will help turn the entire day into a continuous prayer.

READING I   Deut 30:15-20
GOSPEL   Luke 9:22-25

Reading I: Moses sets before his people a program that beautifully describes the purpose and goal of our Lenten life: "Choose life . . . love God, heed his voice."

     Gospel: Jesus lays down a formula for discipleship with him: To be his followers, we must deny ourselves, take up our cross, and follow him.

Beginnings are never easy, especially those that seem to threaten our comfort. Yesterday was Ash Wednesday. It was kind of a spiritual, maybe even emotional, high for us, and now we are face-to-face with seemingly endless weeks of a drab life of penance. Easter seems so far off in the future that the temptation to give up and continue with the old pre-Lenten easy-going religion is very attractive. So we really need the Entrance Antiphon today: "When I cry to the Lord, he hears my voice and saves me from the foes who threaten me." And the psalmist then counsels us: "Unload your burden onto the Lord, and he will support you." Have you ever thought of the Lord as a kind of beast of burden for your cares? But why not, if he himself suggests it?

     The Opening Prayer also deals with beginnings: "Lord, may everything we do begin with your inspiration, continue with your help, and reach perfection *under your guidance.*" We need divine inspiration in order to counteract any mistaken ideas we might have about the nature and purpose of Lent. We know we can do nothing without divine help, and without divine guidance we can all too easily stray from the true goal that Jesus and the Church desire for us during this "day of salvation." One goal is familiar to us from yesterday's liturgy and is repeated today: "Create a clean heart in me, O God; give me a new and steadfast spirit" (Communion Antiphon).

     That "clean heart" might, however, be called the secondary goal of Lent—the one resulting from the primary goal indicated to us by Jesus himself in the Gospel. "The Son of Man must endure many sufferings, be rejected and be put to death, and then be raised up on the third day." Here at the very beginning of Lent, we look off into the distant future—to Good Friday and Easter Sunday, to the making-present-again of the death and resurrection of Jesus and the renewal of our baptismal entrance into that death and resurrection—the true goal of our Lenten life. And then come the words that alone give meaning to Lent: "Whoever wishes to be my follower must deny his very self, take up his cross each day, and follow in my steps."

We said yesterday that the center of religion is not sin, but Christ — following him, living his life. The penitential works we take on, whatever they may be, are not an exercise in self-denial leading possibly to pride of achievement: They make up the cross of Christ, which we willingly and lovingly take upon ourselves. And if a more fervent prayer life, daily or more frequent Mass, some fasting or "giving up" of sweets, drink, or food do not seem terribly important as compared to the cross Jesus carried, we can be certain that the mental, emotional, and physical sufferings that afflict every living being are indeed worthy of comparison to the cross of Jesus. As Mary suffered when she followed her Son, so do we. We might almost make bold to turn the words of the Entrance Antiphon around and say to Jesus: "Unload your burden onto us, and we will support you." We may even find it gratifying to see ourselves as beasts for divine burdens!

But all this may sound a little lugubrious, and that's the last thing we want at this beginning of Lent. There's a lot of brightness and even some good cheer in the First Reading. Moses was a man after the heart of God. He had many weaknesses, not the least of which was a great inferiority complex. God thought more of him than he did of himself. But he eventually convinced Moses that he was the man he wanted to lead his people out of slavery in Egypt into the Promised Land, and today's reading sounds as though the Lord was successful in giving Moses the self-confidence he needed for the work.

"I call heaven and earth today to witness against you," Moses told his people; "I have set before you life and death, the blessing and the curse. CHOOSE LIFE, THEN, that you and your descendants may live, by loving the Lord, your God, heeding his voice, and holding fast to him." Choose life. This is God's will for us now. This is what Lent is all about: choosing life, new life with Christ, Easter life, a new heart within.

* * *

"Unload your burden onto the Lord, and he will support you" *(Entrance Antiphon)*.

"Choose life, then, that you and your descendants may live, by loving the Lord, your God, heeding his voice, and holding fast to him" *(Reading I)*.

"Create a clean heart in me, O God; give me a new and steadfast spirit" *(Communion Antiphon).*

222   FRIDAY AFTER ASH WEDNESDAY

READING I   Isa 58:1-9
GOSPEL   Matt 9:14-15

Reading I: Isaiah sets forth guidelines for fasting. He tells us how *not* to fast and then gives the ideal attitude that will make fasting a blessed experience.

Gospel: Jesus compares his life with the apostles to a wedding celebration during which fasting would be inappropriate. When the bridegroom is taken away, then they can fast.

"Lord, guide the penance we have begun. Help us to persevere with love and sincerity." The Church responds to this prayer with an inspired treatise on the true nature of fasting — one of the most universal of religious practices. The Jews had (and have) their Day of Atonement. Moslems have their Ramadan, and Buddhists fast regularly. So we Christians aren't the only ones. Fasting from food and drink have even been used as a powerful weapon aimed at changing public opinion or disagreeable laws. Mahatma Gandhi used hunger strikes to hasten the independence of India, and in our country Cesar Chavez fasts for a living wage for his farm workers.

In Reading I, Isaiah provides guidelines that can make our Lenten fasting profitable both for us and for our world. Drawing on the sad experience he has had with his people, he warns us: "Your fast ends in quarreling and fighting, striking with wicked claw. Lo, on your fast day you carry out your own pursuits, and drive all your laborers. . . . Is this the manner of fasting I wish . . . ? Do you call this a fast, a day acceptable to the Lord?" We need to be reminded that religious acts, good in themselves, that make us more difficult to live with can hardly be genuinely religious.

Isaiah — speaking the mind of the Lord — insists that fasting has to be related to the life of the community — it has to be social: "This is the fasting that I wish: releasing those bound unjustly, untying the thongs of the yoke . . . . Sharing your bread with the hungry,

clothing the naked . . . and not turning your back on your own."
We Christians have not been too accustomed to this insight into the
nature of fasting, but it is returning. We now regularly hear
religious leaders urging us to give to the poor the money we save by
cutting down on or giving up foods and other pleasures.

It is this kind of fasting that works change — change in the way of
life of the underprivileged, and above all change in ourselves, as
Isaiah indicates: "Then your light shall break forth like the dawn,
and your wound shall quickly be healed . . . . Then you shall call,
and the Lord will answer, you shall cry for help, and he will say:
Here I am!"

The Church chooses Psalm 51 with which to respond to this
treatise on the true nature of fasting. This psalm is essentially a confession of guilt and of sorrow for sins we have committed. By fasting
we discipline physical hungers primarily in order to bring about
broken, contrite hearts which will be fertile soil for the seeding of
God's revivifying love. "My sacrifice, O God, is a contrite spirit; a
heart contrite and humbled, O God, you will not spurn."

In the Gospel Jesus adds another insight into the nature and purpose of fasting. He reminds the disciples of John that fasting at a
wedding reception is unheard of. Consciously or unconsciously, the
disciples recognize that Jesus is the long-awaited bridegroom of the
messianic kingdom, Israel's true spouse, and it is simply inconceiv-
able that they should fast while he is still with them. The time will
come when he will be taken away from them, and then they will
fast.

It is significant that this Gospel is used today. Six weeks from today will be Good Friday when Jesus, the divine bridegroom, will be
taken away from the disciples by death. Then they can fast and their
fasting will be an expression of longing desire for him and his return.
And this is our situation now. Our fasting makes us hungry, makes
us thirsty, not only for human food and drink, but most of all it
sharpens our hunger for Jesus, who in himself, in his person, is the
only food that can satisfy these yearning hearts of ours. "Seek good
and not evil so that you may live, and the Lord will be with you"
(Gospel Verse).

* * *

"A broken, humbled heart, O God, you will not scorn" (Responsorial Psalm).

"This is the fasting that I wish: Sharing your bread with the hungry, sheltering the oppressed and the homeless" *(Reading I)*.

"Teach us your ways, O Lord, and lead us in your paths" *(Communion Antiphon)*.

223   SATURDAY AFTER ASH WEDNESDAY

READING I   Isa 58:9-14
GOSPEL   Luke 5:27-32

Reading I: Isaiah describes in vivid terms the glory of a sinner who has allowed the Lord to restore his heart. He will take delight in the Lord and the Lord in him.

Gospel: Jesus is accused of associating with tax collectors and sinners, and he in turn gives his reasons for preferring their company.

Today's Gospel is a perfect illustration of the point we have been insisting on — that the center of Christianity is not sin but Christ who has conquered sin and death, Christ who calls us out of sin to new life with him. He does this by being present to and with us, even as he was present in Levi's house to that crowd of sinners and unsavory characters, "non-observers of the law," according to the judgment of the professionally religious people called the Pharisees and the scribes. Jesus feels at home with them — they are his kind of people — and obviously they like him and feel comfortable with him.

In answering his critics Jesus clearly indicates his reasons for preferring this sort of company: "The healthy do not need a doctor; sick people do. I have not come to invite the self-righteous to a change of heart, but sinners." "Jesus Christ, M.D." — that's the way he describes himself. Or more exactly, "Jesus Christ, Heart Specialist," for his healing has to do more with sick hearts than sick bodies. His preferred patients are those who realize that they are ill and really want to be healed, not the self-righteous Pharisees who are convinced of their spiritual well-being, because, after all, aren't they the ones who have fullfilled all the prescriptions of the law?

Our Lord's language here is full of deep meaning. He uses terms like "invite" and "change of heart." God has made his people free; he does not force himself on anyone, for that would be doing violence to the freedom he gave to his children. All he can do is present himself to them as the totally desirable one—as Jesus does at Levi's house (and to us always), and leave the decision and choice to them. He becomes the occasion of grace to them, and when they see him, they respond by offering their hearts to him. He in turn operates on the hearts and makes them like unto his own. This mutual exchange of hearts—isn't that what salvation means? Isn't that the purpose of Lent? Isn't it also the purpose of the sacrament of reconciliation (which we used to call the sacrament of Penance)? The essential point is that Jesus is both the surgeon and the donor.

We need not stretch our imaginations too far to see the reception and dinner at Levi's house as a "preview" of the Mass. At Mass the same Jesus who ate and drank with Levi's sinful friends eats and drinks and speaks with us. Here, too, he forgives our sins, and if our hearts are seriously diseased by sin and there is need of a major operation—a heart transplant—he best takes care of that in his own "operating room," the sacrament of reconciliation.

In Reading I Isaiah depicts in attractive human terms the delight that God takes in a sinner who has allowed Christ to give him or her that heart transplant he speaks about in the Gospel. Changing the imagery a bit, the darkness of sin gives way to light, bright as the midday. "Then the Lord will guide you always and give you plenty even on the parched land. He will renew your strength, and you shall be like a watered garden, like a spring whose water never fails."

"Light shall rise for you in the darkness," says Isaiah. Six weeks from tonight we will celebrate Christ's resurrection. The Easter candle, representing the risen Christ, will enter the darkened church, and we shall all receive new light from it, symbolic of the new hearts the Doctor will give us. Easter water will be blessed, and we will all be sprinkled with it and become that "watered garden . . . whose water never fails" (Reading I). And Isaiah tells us how we will feel about this: "Then you shall take delight in the Lord, and I will make you ride on the heights of the earth."

So here, at the beginning of Lent, Jesus, having diagnosed all our weaknesses and wounds, sends us this invitation: "Follow me. I do not wish the sinner to die but to turn to me and live" (Gospel Verse). But the healing is not going to be instant. There has to be considerable "prepping" for the surgery. And that's what Lent is all about— Lent, with all its obligations, its repentance, its spiritual growing up and turning our lives around. New hearts require a new way of life.

And for that Isaiah in Reading I provides a good prescription: "Remove from your midst oppression, false accusation and malicious speech . . . bestow your bread on the hungry, and satisfy the afflicted." But few people would care to face a serious operation like a heart transplant without God's help, and so we pray: "Father, look upon our weakness and reach out to help us with your loving power."

* * *

"Teach me your way, O Lord, that I may be faithful in your sight" *(Responsorial Psalm)*.

"I do not wish the sinner to die, says the Lord, but to turn to me and live" *(Gospel Verse)*.

"It is mercy I want, and not sacrifice, says the Lord; I did not come to call the virtuous, but sinners" *(Communion Antiphon)*.

22   FIRST SUNDAY OF LENT   Cycle A

READING I Gen 2:7-9; 3:1-7   **READING II**   Rom 5:12-19
GOSPEL   Matt 4:1-11

Reading I: We hear the account of the Fall of Adam and Eve. They yield to the temptation to want to be like God. They forget their dependency on the Creator, and their eyes are opened.

Reading II: St. Paul describes the meaning of the Fall and the contrast between the disobedience of the first Adam and the obedience of Christ, the second Adam.

Gospel: Here is described the forty-day fast of Jesus in the desert followed by his victorious resistance against the temptations of Satan.

How have we developed in our understanding of Lent? Most of us have probably seen it as a personal contest with our lower nature — an effort to control our appetites — that had little connection with the Church as such and even less with the death and resurrection of Christ.

So, too, our baptism: It was something done to us that, of course, we don't remember unless we were converts to the Catholic faith. We may get some insight into the meaning of our baptism when we renew our baptismal vows on Holy Saturday night, but for the most part it has probably not conditioned our lives or in any way provided us with any guidelines for life since it happened.

Today's Mass texts provide us with a real opportunity to arrive at a deeper understanding of the full reality of life and in particular of our life as Christians. And don't be alarmed if I say that the texts contain a rather deep lesson in theology. What is life all about? It's an understatement to say that it is full of mystery. But far from discouraging thought, mystery invites us to deeper speculation and insight. So, if we would like a better understanding of the mystery of life, of history, of our present world, to say nothing of our own persons, this Mass is what we are looking for.

The First Reading, for example, provides us with an understanding of our human condition and, in particular, how we got the way we are. The Lord God creates, gives being to, the first man and the first woman. He makes them "in his own likeness," that is, he gives them the power to think, to reason, to reflect, to choose, to love. Above all, he makes them free, as he is free, and he gives them an opportunity to exercise their freedom by choosing to obey his command not to eat of the fruit of one particular tree. It is a command that is to remind them forever that *they are creatures* and that they are totally dependent on him for everything that they are and have, for he is *Creator*, he is Lord of all.

We know what happened: They are tempted to deny their origin, their dependency on God, and their refusal to remember is what we know of as the Fall. It is a sin that contains in germ all of human history—with all its sadness, its misery, pain, sorrow, anguish, corruption. This was the first entrance of evil into creation, and every sin since that day repeats and adds to the sum total of evil that involves us all. When I sin, I ratify Adam's sin. I share in the sinful human condition that originated with him and make it my own. St. Paul puts it this way in Reading II: "Sin entered the world through one man, and through sin, death, and thus death has spread through the whole human race because everyone has sinned." Those last words need emphasis.

This is the background against which we can acquire some insight into what is going on around us now in our world, what is going on in us. "Be merciful, O Lord, for we have sinned. Against you only have I sinned, and done what is evil in your sight" (Responsorial Psalm).

Now we may wonder what difference Christ has made and continues to make in that sad picture. The incident in today's Gospel informs us beautifully. The event takes place right after his baptism when he submits his life to the Father, and the Father proclaims him as his beloved Son in whom he is well pleased. Immediately after that divine pronouncement, the Holy Spirit leads him into the desert where, after forty days of fasting, he is tempted by Satan.

The temptations are real. They make it clear that Jesus is fully human, and we must not be afraid to admit that he was fully human, that his humanity was not a kind of masquerade that he wore. And the fact of his being tempted is entirely compatible with his divinity and his sinlessness. The temptations are different and yet perhaps just variations on the one great single temptation: to declare himself independent of the Father, to take back the obedience implicit in his submission to the Father at his baptism.

The contrast or parallel with the first Adam is perfect. The first Adam was disobedient, he refused to serve, he wanted to be like God. Now, at the end of the third temptation, Jesus cries, "Away with you, Satan! Scripture says: 'You shall do homage to the Lord your God; him alone shall you adore.'"

What meaning does all this have for us? For one thing, we can say that Jesus lived our entire lifetime in those forty days in the desert. In our own way we experience the same temptations he did. Do I want to live for myself instead of for others? Do I do things for my own self-glorification as the devil wanted Jesus to do? or for the enrichment of the lives of others, as Jesus did during his lifetime? Is my life a constant competing with others for honor and recognition, for rewards and prestige? Do I hurt others by word or attitude? What efforts do I make to choose the Father's will as my own?

Jesus actually overcame all our temptations for us, in our name. But like the whole redemptive act itself, his victory will not be ours unless and until we make it our own. We do enter into the death and resurrection of Christ in our baptism. His victory is ours, even as his death is. But our baptism has to be lived out all our lives, or to put it another way, life is simply our day-by-day, year-by-year progressive possessing of the dying and rising of Christ, of his victory over Satan. His victory will not be ours unless we make it our own, and this has to be a deliberate, freely chosen decision on our part.

There is another element in today's Gospel that has meaning for us. It is to be found in those forty days of fasting and solitude that Jesus spent in the desert. God speaks to him as he spoke to his people Israel through the prophet Hosea: "I will allure her; I will lead her into the desert and speak to her heart" (Hos 2:16). That promise is fulfilled again now, during this Lent, *in us.* To us God says: "I will allure you; I will lead you into the desert and speak to your heart."

Lent is more than anything else a time for God to speak to our hearts. Jesus' victory over Satan was forged by forty days of listening with his heart to the voice of the Father and in responding to that voice. So, too, God willing, will our victory be prepared during this Lent.

So the best way for us to personalize, to ratify and make our own, Christ's victory over Satan and over our fallen nature is to do what Jesus did: Listen—listen to the voice of the Father, listen with our ears, with our minds, our hearts, our whole being. With that kind of listening, no evil shall befall us, for God will give his angels charge over us and guard us in all our ways. "Man does not live on bread alone, but on every word that comes from the mouth of God" (Communion Verse).

* * *

"Be merciful, O Lord, for we have sinned" *(Responsorial Psalm).*

"The Lord will overshadow you, and you will find refuge under his wings" *(Communion Antiphon).*

23   FIRST SUNDAY OF LENT   Cycle B

READING I Gen 9:8-15   **READING II** 1 Pet 3:18-22
GOSPEL Matt 1:12-15

Reading I: After saving Noah and his family from the flood, God establishes a covenant with him. The rainbow will be a constant reminder of the covenant.

Reading II: St. Peter compares baptism to the rescue of Noah and his family.

Gospel: Mark gives a brief account of Jesus' temptations and the beginning of his preaching.

It is difficult for adult Christians to get excited about their baptism. Most of them were baptized as babies, and that was that. We advance from one stage in life to another: we leave infancy behind, we leave childhood behind . . . and then adolescence. *But we never leave baptism behind.* It is always with us, shaping, directing, inspiring our lives. One purpose of Lent is to help us grow in an ever deeper understanding of what baptism can mean for us here and now and in the years ahead. The Christian life is baptism lived out. It is as simple as that, but if we don't realize what baptism really is, how can we live it out? Lent asks us to renew our baptism and get going into a new, fresh start in being shaped by it.

The original purpose of Lent was the final preparation of the catechumens (prospective converts) for their reception into the Christian community, the Body of Christ, through baptism. The Lenten Mass readings are full of signs and symbols that point to and clarify the meaning of baptism and the community into which the catechumens are to be received. We can be sure that the readings also intensified the hunger and thirst of the prospective Christians for the loving union with Jesus and their fellow Christians that baptism was to bring them.

Today's First Reading takes us back to Noah and the great flood, and, most important of all, the covenant-alliance God made with Noah and his family. These few people floated safely over the flood waters in the ark (a symbol of the Church), and Peter, in Reading II, which was originally a baptismal sermon, tells the candidates: "You are now saved by a baptismal bath which corresponds to this [the ark] exactly. This baptism is no removal of physical stain, but the pledge of God of an irreproachable conscience through the resurrection of Jesus Christ."

Having saved Noah and his family from the flood, God established a covenant with him and his descendants. The sign of that covenant was a rainbow. Thereafter, every time the people saw a rainbow in the skies they were reminded of their covenant-agreement of love with the saving God. Joining heaven and earth as it does with beautiful colors, God could not have chosen a more appropriate symbol. Is there any reason why the rainbows we see (they are all too few) should not remind us, too, of our love agreement with our God which we entered upon at our baptism? May we not even consider Lent a rainbow made up of signs and words?

But Lent has always been more than a final preparation of the catechumens. It is for the entire community, who originally felt involved in preparing the catechumens; everyone entered into the spirit of the preparation. Praying and fasting with the catechumens, they saw the forty days of Lent as a time of spiritual renewal for the entire parish.

How are we today to understand these Lenten readings and Lent itself? As already indicated, we simply cannot dismiss the ancient readings, chants, and prayers as having no meaning for us, as we may have done in the past when many looked on Lent as a strictly personal and private experience in self-conquest or as a time for bettering our private prayer. It is a time for personal conversion, to be sure, but it is much more. It is a summons to the entire community and to the universal Church to a renewed vision of what it really is as the Body of Christ. Lent "is a time of choice, when the community is summoned to return to God," says Fr. Adrian Nocent, O.S.B. (*The Liturgical Year*, vol. 2 [Lent], Collegeville, Minn.: The Liturgical Press, 1977, 36).

Today Jesus says *to us:* "This is the time of fulfillment. The reign of God is at hand! Reform your lives and believe in the good news!" But the community is made up of us as individuals, and it is we, each of us, who bears the responsibility of the community's conversion. Conversion begins with the call of Christ addressed to each and to all, aimed at our inmost being, our heart. Confronted with this call, the heart has to declare its intentions and dispositions.

So, a purely intellectual change—a deeper knowledge, a change of ideas about Christ, about the Church is not enough. So too is a conversion that would involve only religious sentiment or emotion, or even one that would change a person's ethical behavior. It is with one's deepest being, with all that constitutes an adult, mature person —in a word, with one's heart—that the believer assumes his position in the presence of the challenging Christ. The human heart welcomes Christ and his word and becomes a heart indwelled by Jesus. Paul's prayer for his Ephesians is fulfilled here and now: "That Christ may dwell in your hearts through faith . . . that you may be filled with all the fulness of God" (3:17-19).

Many modern Christians speak of actually *experiencing* Jesus in a very vivid sort of encounter that thenceforth changed their lives. That's the way it was with St. Paul. Whether or not such a dramatic experience of Jesus is to be expected or can be arranged is open to question. I suspect that the more ordinary way to conversion is more like that of a man and woman who gradually come to know each other over a period of time and eventually fall in love. And so too our yearly experiencing of Jesus and his power in experiences like Lent and Advent.

What we must insist on is that it is conversion to Christ—to Christ in person, who is real and living now, Christ who is asking us personally and as a community to accept him into our lives, into our judging and our evaluating. This means accepting, and totally committing ourselves to, the world of Jesus Christ's judgments and values. It means welcoming into our hearts a new mentality, that of Christ himself. The result is the reshaping of our whole existence; it means total adhering to Jesus as our Lord and Savior.

But we may not forget that the Christ to whom we adhere is the *whole* Christ — not only his teaching but also the continuation of himself which he called Church and St. Paul called his Body. You can't have Christ, the whole Christ, without having or wanting to have Christ's Church and its actualization in a community, a parish. Nor can we love Christ without also loving one another. "If we love one another God dwells in us, and his love is brought to perfection in us" (1 John 4).

This, all of it, is the Good News that Jesus asks us to accept today and make our own.

* * *

"Your ways, O Lord, are truth and love, to those who keep your covenant" *(Responsorial Psalm).*

"The reign of God is at hand! Reform your lives and believe in the good news" *(Gospel).*

"The Lord will overshadow you, and you will find refuge under his wings" *(Communion Verse).*

24   **FIRST SUNDAY OF LENT**   Cycle C

READING I Deut 26:4-10   READING II Rom 10:8-13
GOSPEL   Luke 4:1-13

Reading I: This reading tells of how the Hebrews went to Egypt, grew into a great nation, were oppressed and delivered from captivity by God's strong hand.

Reading II: Expressed here is the confession of faith that Jesus is Lord who died and was raised from the dead by the power of God.

Gospel: The reading gives details of the three temptations of Jesus at the beginning of his public life.

Today's liturgy is the overture of Lent; it is the entire holy season in miniature. Actually, it is our entire Christian life as individuals and as the Church, as our parish community, in miniature.

In the past most Christians have looked upon Lent primarily as a personal and individual experience, a call to individual sinners to repent and be converted. It is that, surely, but more than anything else Lent has a communal meaning. It is the experience of an entire people as a people. And, it is the Church herself in today's readings that seeks to bring this truth home to us.

The First Reading has to do with a people—the people of God headed by Moses which, we Christians believe, prefigures the people of God, the Church, headed by Jesus Christ. It has to do with the people's finding its identity, coming to terms with its weaknesses and strengths, above all, coming to know itself as the people in whom God takes his delight. It sums up all of Jewish history to the moment of the entry into the Promised Land.

This text from Deuteronomy has been called the most important passage in the whole Old Testament. The key ideas are that "the Lord heard our voice and saw our misery, our toil and our oppression; the Lord brought us out of Egypt . . . with signs and wonders. He brought us here and gave us this land." Therefore, the people bring to the Lord the first fruits of the products of the soil which the Lord gave them, thereby recognizing his lordship over them. We should note the emphasis on the fact that it is the *Lord* and he alone who has done everything for his people. This, too, is the main idea of the Second Reading and indeed of all of Paul's letters. The Exodus was the foundation experience that formed a slave people into God's people, thereby establishing their identity as that people.

It is quite easy to establish that we as a Church now experience and share in the great model-experiences of God's people on their way to the Promised Land. As they were pilgrims, so are we a pilgrim people. And Lent is our time par excellence for remembering the Jewish experience and its meaning in our lives. But Jesus had this experience, too. Notice the words of the Gospel: "Jesus, full of the Holy Spirit, returned from the Jordan and was led by the Spirit into the desert for forty days, where he was tempted by the devil." Those forty days have deep meaning. How often he must have thought of his people's forty years of wandering in the desert. And he must surely have realized that he was making their experiences, hardships, and temptations his very own. But he was also making our experiences, hardships, and temptations his own.

After eating nothing for forty days, Jesus was hungry. It was real hunger, just as the devil's temptations were real temptations.

Because we believe that Jesus is the Son of God, we may have imagined that the temptations were a kind of play-acting, that Jesus was in some way above all that human experience, that he was just allowing the devil to make these tempting suggestions so that he could put him in his place. The author of the Book of Hebrews disagrees: "We do not have a high priest who is unable to sympathize with our weakness, but one who was tempted in every way that we are, yet never sinned. . . . He is able to deal patiently with erring sinners. . . . Son though he was, he learned obedience from what he suffered" (4:15; 5:2, 8).

The temptations were not only real, they were subtle, mainly because, like most temptations, they were disguised in the appearance of good. Turn stones into bread. Why not? If he could do that, he could some day feed his hungry people, provide unlimited supplies of food stamps for them. Again, why not take over all the kingdoms of the world and so satisfy the legitimate patriotic longings of his oppressed people for a homeland of their own. Finally, why not jump off the parapet of the Temple? After all, the devil argues, if you are God's son, he has to be on your side. Don't you have any faith in God's own words. You are going to demand faith of your followers, show some yourself . . . now!

Jesus resists all the temptations, but I doubt that he had an easier time than the rest of us do. What he actually accomplishes here is that he establishes a priority of spiritual values for himself, for his own life, for the life of his Church, for us. And he does it in the light of the experience and even the terminology of the Old Testament people of God: "Scripture has it, 'Not on bread alone shall man live.'" "You shall do homage to the Lord your God; him alone shall you adore." "You shall not put the Lord your God to the test."

So for Jesus there are forty days of fasting in the desert, days of communing with the Father, ending in temptation, but temptation is swallowed up in victory. Here at the beginning of his public life he determines his way—a path that will lead him through work, disappointment, anger, grief, betrayal, pain, and finally disgraceful death. But we recall the ancient symbol of the phoenix—the mythical bird of the Egyptian desert that rises up gloriously out of its own ashes. Christ is going to be consumed by death, but he will rise again and live forever. And so, too, we who are his followers.

Jesus lived our lifetime in that desert. His temptations are ours now. Do I want to live for myself instead of for others? Do I do things for my own glorification or to enrich the lives of others? Is my life a constant competing with others for honor and recognition, for rewards and prestige? Do I overindulge my appetites? Do I seek the will of the Father or my own?

Jesus overcame all our temptations for us, in our name. But like the whole redeeming act itself, his victory will not be ours unless we seek to make it our own. We cannot overcome temptations, even the tiniest, without God's help and grace. But we have to want that help, we have to position ourselves to receive it.

Today's liturgy brings to mind the words God spoke through the prophet Hosea: "So I will allure her; I will lead her into the desert and speak to her heart" (2:16). So did the Lord speak to his people Israel and so does he speak to us. During this desert experience of Lent, God will speak tenderly to us, reminding us who we are, and to what we are called, what must have first priority in our lives. Above all, he will tell us again and again how great is his love for us. Then we will know who we are; we will know that we are his very own people in whom he takes delight.

The purpose of religion, above all, of Lent, is not to scare people into being ethical or pious. It is rather to help them grow in loving intimacy with and gratitude to Jesus who has done, and continues to do, such great things for us.

* * *

"Be with me, Lord, when I am in trouble" *(Responsorial Psalm)*.

"Man does not live on bread alone but on every word that comes from the mouth of God" *(Gospel)*.

"The Lord will overshadow you, and you will find refuge under his wings" *(Communion Antiphon)*.

225 MONDAY OF THE FIRST WEEK OF LENT

READING I Lev 19:1-2, 11-18
GOSPEL Matt 25:31-46

Reading I: God proposes an ideal of holiness which is arrived at by refraining from injuring our neighbor in any way.

Gospel: Jesus tells us that our eternal destiny depends on the manner and degree of the care and help we give to the poor and underprivileged.

We are definitely off now. Lent has really begun. It begins with a program for us proposed by God himself: "Speak to the whole Israelite community and tell them: Be holy, for I, the Lord, your God, am holy." Deeper holiness, more evident godliness, is the aim of Lent for us and for the whole Church. Is that the way we have customarily thought of Lent?

That same objective is proposed to us by Jesus in the Gospel, although in somewhat different terms. Jesus describes the last judgment in graphic images. The criterion by which we will be judged will be whether or not we have fed the hungry, given drink to the thirsty, visited the imprisoned — in a word, whether or not we have been merciful, kind, caring in all our relationships with those who are in pain or trouble of any kind, regardless of whether we know them or not.

So our relationship with God, our personal holiness, and our eternal destiny depend entirely on our relationship with our neighbor. "Your words, Lord, are spirit and life" (Responsorial Psalm). God tells us to be holy, but he knows very well that we cannot create his holiness within ourselves. But by observing the ideal he proposes to us, we can condition our hearts for the holiness which he will then be willing to share with us. "The law of the Lord is perfect, refreshing the soul; the precepts of the Lord are right, rejoicing the heart."

There is no escaping the questions that these demands make us face up to. How do we feel and think and speak about our neighbor? When was the last time we injured anyone by spreading slander? Do we cherish grudges, desire revenge, bear hatred in our hearts towards anyone? In what ways do we measure up to the ideal of positive charity proposed to us in the Gospel? "Those who are indifferent to human suffering are just as guilty as those who inflict it." I don't know who wrote that, but it is surely an exact corollary of the Gospel.

Not only does Jesus accuse us in the Gospel, but he raises up women and men whose presence in our time is a never-ending accusation. Today's Gospel could be called the constitution of the lifework of Mother Teresa and her followers. Does it not seem strange that she is so widely acclaimed simply because she is doing what Jesus asked all his followers to do? Is real Christianity all that rare? There is no doubt: She is a presence in the world and to the world — a presence of grace that challenges us all at the very core of our Christian observance.

We are not claiming that all Christians have to live in exactly the same way as Mother Teresa. But Jesus in the Gospel and Jesus present in Teresa's life and work does demand of us a new, personalized *attitude* towards all the poor and underprivileged — physically or psychologically, including those in our own midst. The least we can do is open our eyes and hearts to them, and that should not be too difficult if we remind ourselves again and again that we may be seeing hungry, dirty, raggedly-clothed bodies, but the one we are really looking at is Jesus himself. "I assure you," he tells us, "as often as you did it for one of my least brothers, you did it for me." And we may not forget his other conclusion: "As often as you neglected to do it to one of these least ones, you neglected to do it to me."

Now do we understand a little more about what Lent is all about? Lent is to make us holy, it is to make us thoughtful, mindful of human needs; it is to make us into other Christs, possessed of his mind and heart. But oh, how we need help! "As the eyes of servants are on the hands of their master, so our eyes are fixed on the Lord our God, pleading for his mercy. Have mercy on us, Lord, have mercy" (Entrance Antiphon).

* * *

"Your words, O Lord, are spirit and life" *(Responsorial Psalm)*.

"Anything you did for the least of my brothers, you did for me, says the Lord" *(Communion Antiphon)*.

226 TUESDAY OF THE FIRST WEEK OF LENT

READING I Isa 55:10-11
GOSPEL Matt 6:7-15

Reading I: God, through Isaiah, compares his word to the rain and snow that water the earth and make it fertile. Human hearts rise up to God when fertilized by God's word.

Gospel: Jesus gives us a lesson in prayer by sharing with us his own prayer, the Our Father.

Today we learn another of Lent's purposes, perhaps the best of all. The Opening Prayer instructs us: "Father, look on us, your children.

Through the discipline of Lent help us to grow in our desire for you." If at Easter our desire for God is more intense, more demanding, we shall know that our Lent this year has been a success.

But what nourishes desire for God more than his own word? The more we know about him, the greater will be our eagerness to possess and be possessed by him who is love in person. The desire for God is unlike any other desire. It is its own reward, its own fulfillment, but not quite. We are satiated, but we still yearn for more. Infinite abysses in human hearts demand infinite satisfaction, which is a task that only endless eternity can really gratify.

We preface this prayer with the words, "Through the discipline of Lent help us grow . . . ." This is very instructive. Discipline involves labor, it requires self-control, study. The discipline of Lent includes the traditional works—prayer, fasting, almsgiving; but I suggest another: the serious effort to get at the meaning of and meditate on the texts of the Lenten Masses and then reflecting on them during the day.

The prophet Isaiah today provides us with a glorious description of what can happen to us when God's word becomes our daily nourishment. He compares the word of God to the rain and snow that refresh the land, make it fertile, and give life to the seeds planted there. In the same way God wants his word to refresh our hearts and fertilize the seeds of desire for him that we so need. The Lord becomes specific about the hopes he has for our absorbing of his word: "It shall not return to me void, but shall do my will, achieving the end for which I sent it." Our response to God's word planted in our hearts is the best kind of prayer—the kind that gives expression to our desire for God.

If we have difficulty developing our own response to the word, the inspired psalmist can be our greatest help, as, for example, in today's Responsorial Psalm:

> "Glorify the Lord with me,
>   let us together extol his name.
> I sought the Lord, and he answered me
>   and delivered me from all my fears.
> Look to him that you may be radiant with joy . . . .

But the best is yet to come. In the Gospel Jesus tells us that what matters is not the *quantity* of our responses to God's words to us; it is the *quality*. It is not *what* we say or think when we pray, it is *how* we say or think what is in our hearts. Better even than the psalmist, Jesus, God's Son, knows how to respond to the Father's word coming to us through Scripture, through the great sacrament of nature, through anything that is good and beautiful. Remember how we prayed in the Opening Prayer: "Father, look on us, your children . . . ." He looks at us, and we look at him, with Jesus' own prayer on our lips and in our hearts:

> Our Father in heaven,
> hallowed be your name,
> your kingdom come,
> your will be done
> on earth as it is in heaven. . . .
> Give us today our daily bread
> and forgive us the wrong we have done
> as we forgive those who wrong us.
> Subject us not to the trial
> but deliver us from the evil one.

And Jesus goes on to warn us immediately that prayer of praise to the Father and of petition for our needs is no prayer at all unless in our hearts we are willing to forgive anyone who has offended us.

It has been said that the Lord's Prayer is the summary of the Gospel. It is Jesus' own prayer, so it has to be the perfect prayer. It comes from his heart; it is his personal response to all that the Father is and says to him.

So in today's Mass God looks on us his children; he speaks to us and his word echoes in our hearts and minds. The echo reaches back to him as our prayer, and the ultimate result cannot be anything but growth in desire for God. "In every age, O Lord, you have been our refuge. From all eternity, you are God" (Entrance Antiphon).

* * *

"From all their afflictions God will deliver the just" *(Responsorial Psalm).*

"Take pity on me, Lord, and hear my prayer" *(Communion Antiphon).*

READING I   Jonah 3:1-10
GOSPEL   Luke 11:29-32

Reading I: Jonah preaches penance to the Ninevites, and they respond by recognizing their sinfulness. They proclaim a fast as the sign of their desire to return to God.

Gospel: Jesus presents the contrast between the Ninevites' return to God and the unwillingness of Jesus' contemporaries to heed his call to repentance.

The Ninevites are made aware of their sinfulness and their need to return to God by the preaching of Jonah. Jonah's very presence was grace to them. Such was not the case with the "evil age" to which Jesus preached repentance. He was rejected by most of his hearers. We can imagine the sadness in his voice when he complained: "The queen of the south will rise in judgment along with the men of this generation, and she will condemn them. She came from the farthest corner of the world to lisen to the wisdom of Solomon, but you have a greater than Solomon here." The Ninevites were converted by Jonah's preaching. Jesus is God's own Son, but his contemporaries reject him.

It's quite a mystery — that Jonah, a mere man, and a reluctant prophet — was able to bring an entire city back to God. But Jesus, who is God in person, fails. What can we make of this? Maybe we can just settle for the perverseness of fallen human nature — our unwillingness to respond to divine goodness, even when, at times, we recognize it. Sin itself is a mystery. We know what harm it does to ourselves and to others, yet we deliberately choose to commit it. Would we have been converted by the preaching of Jesus? Does his presence to us now in the Gospel bring us back to him? Why is it that year after year we need the preaching, not only of Jesus but of John the Baptist and the prophets as well?

I suspect that part of Jonah's effectiveness resulted from the kind of motivation he inspired. He *scared* the Ninevites into conversion: "Forty days more and Nineveh shall be destroyed." Inspired by fear or not, the conversion was genuine, and the Lord God "saw *by their actions* how they turned from their evil away," and he received them back into his forgiving heart. Those words, "he saw by their actions," are very revealing. The Ninevites' fasting was a sign to God, an indication of their willingness to return to God, along with their desire to receive him back into their lives.

All this throws light on our own Lenten life, and it provides a context for the kinds of mortification we take upon ourselves. It also makes us examine our motives for these Lenten practices. We don't have to observe a strict fast, as in the old days. But the Church will never give up telling her people of the serious need for self-discipline in their lives. She knows that if we do not control our appetites, they will control us and deprive us of our humanity. But if the self-discipline of the Christian is not an act of love and does not make us desire God more, it can easily lead to self-glorification and vanity and thus defeat its own true purpose.

"With all your heart turn to me," says the Lord, "for I am tender and compassionate" (Gospel Verse). "Lord, look upon us and hear our prayer. By the good works you inspire, help us to discipline our bodies and to be renewed in spirit" (Opening Prayer).

It is noteworthy that the Church has us respond to the story of the Ninevites' conversion by putting into our hearts and mouths the familiar old penitential Psalm 51: "Have mercy on me, O God, in your goodness; in the greatness of your compassion wipe out my offense. . . . A clean heart create for me, O God, and a steadfast spirit renew within me. . . . My sacrifice, O God, is a contrite spirit; a heart contrite and humbled, O God, you will not spurn."

* * *

"Remember your mercies, Lord, your tenderness from ages past" (Entrance Antiphon).

"A broken, humbled heart, O God, you will not scorn" (Responsorial Psalm).

"With all your heart turn to me for I am tender and compassionate" (Gospel Verse).

READING I   Esth C:12, 14-16, 23-25
GOSPEL   Matt 7:7-12

Reading I: Queen Esther presents a beautiful lesson in prayer.

Gospel: Jesus' prayer likewise teaches about prayer, with special emphasis on perseverance in prayer.

Prayer, along with fasting and almsgiving, is a traditional Lenten work for Christians. The three go together, complement each other, and all aim at renewal of the human heart, increasing our desire for God. "Let my words reach your ears, Lord; listen to my groaning, and hear the cry of my prayer, O my King and my God" (Entrance Antiphon).

Prayer always begins with God—with his inspiring us to address him whenever we decide to pray. But prayer primarily is not what we say to God; it is what God says to us *and* our response to his word. That word comes to us in Scripture, in the liturgy, and very specially in the great sacrament or sign which we call nature. There is no limit to the ways in which God communicates himself to us so that we can experience him and respond to him.

All this is illustrated in the structure of the Mass itself. We hear God speaking to us in the readings from Scripture, and we respond with words of thanks and praise: "Thanks be to God!" and "Praise to you, Lord Jesus Christ!" Better still, after Reading I, we respond to God's word with his own inspired word from the psalms: "Lord, on the day I called for help, you answered me. I will give thanks to you, O Lord, with all my heart" (Responsorial Psalm). The psalm usually echoes the main ideas of the reading, and we can make those echoes our own and add a few personal hopes, desires, and needs to what the psalm says.

Today's First Reading is itself a magnificent prayer, as well as a useful lesson in how to pray. Queen Esther begins with a recognition of the majesty and supremacy of God: "My Lord, my King, you alone are God." The glory of God is her first concern; the entire first half recalls and rejoices in that glory. It is only after she has positioned herself in the presence of the Lord that she presumes to present her petitions, the needs of her people first and then her own: "Help me, who am alone and have no one but you, O Lord. You know all things."

Indeed, God does know all things, he is aware of our needs without our telling him, but, as Queen Esther reminds us, we are his children, and as children, it is perfectly natural for us to ask our Father for what we need. "Be mindful of us, O Lord. Manifest yourself in the time of our distress and give me courage." How could God resist that kind of praying? He couldn't and didn't.

Jesus also instructs us in how to pray. He says: Just do it. "Ask, and you will receive. Knock and it will be opened to you. For the one who asks, receives." He then goes on to tell us the reason for the kind of daring optimism he recommends: God is our Father. Fathers love their children and care for them. "If you, with all your sins, know how to give your children what is good, how much more will your heavenly Father give good things to anyone who asks him."

Lent is a good time for us to re-examine our prayer life, and we can't find a better pattern for this examination than today's readings. We can never be satisfied with our praying, and that is as it should be. One of our problems is that we do not take Christ sufficiently at his word. We do not believe enough in the Father's love for us. Nor do we believe enough in our own worth, as Esther did.

Another problem is that we so often lack success in praying, in getting our requests granted. We pray but nothing happens. But Jesus tells us — and it may be the main lesson of today's Gospel — don't give up. Don't give up on the Father, because the Father does not give up on you. You may not immediately receive the favor you are asking for. Neither did Jesus himself, when he prayed in the Garden, begging the Father to deliver him from the Passion. The Father gave him the Passion but also something else — the resurrection and his glorification. And more than all else, he gave him *our* redemption. In some mysterious way our praying, especially in moments of darkness and dismay, places us in the garden with Christ. I can't think of a better place to be.

* * *

"Let my words reach your ears, Lord; listen to my groaning, and hear the cry of my prayer, O my King, my God" *(Entrance Antiphon)*.

"Lord, on the day I called for help, you answered me" *(Responsorial Psalm)*.

"Everyone who asks will receive; whoever seeks shall find, and to him who knocks it shall be opened" *(Communion Antiphon)*.

READING I   Ezek 18:21-28
GOSPEL   Matt 5:20-26

Reading I: Ezechiel speaks of God's forgiveness to sinners who repent and warns the virtuous people who depart from the path of virtue to do evil.

Gospel: Jesus tells us that worship of God can be ruined by unwillingness to be reconciled with anyone who has anything against us.

"By my life, I do not wish the sinner to die, says the Lord, but to turn to me and live" (Communion Antiphon).

That simple verse from Ezechiel sums up the entire Bible, not to mention the life of our Lord and the purpose of Lent. It is one of life's mysteries that so many of us seem unable to believe what the Lord tells us: "I do not wish the death of the sinner . . . ." Some seem to think their sins are so great that God cannot forgive them. The Responsorial Psalm cries to God: "If you, O Lord, laid bare our guilt, who could endure it?" Well, we may not be able to endure it, but the Lord has no problem with it.

This is the main message of the First Reading today. The Lord tells us through the prophet Ezechiel: "If the wicked man turns away from all the sins he committed, if he keeps all my statutes and does what is right and just, he shall surely live, he shall not die. . . ." Lent is indeed a time for repentance and sorrow for past sins. But repentance is more than mere regret springing from a sense of self-defeat. Lent is a time for conversion, of a real change of mind and heart, a time for all to learn to think, to judge, and to live our community life as *totally responsible human beings.*

The element of responsibility in his children is terribly important for God. Growing up, becoming responsible, is the real meaning of conversion. That could well be the message of the second part of Reading I. Actually, the reading may shock us. God seems almost overly anxious to forgive the wicked person who repents, but he is simply intractable about the virtuous one who "turns from the path of virtue to do evil." I do believe that God is more than eager to forgive any repentant sinner, but what he may be warning against here is the total lack of responsibility in the virtuous man who forsakes God for his own self-glorification. The sinner is weak; he may be ignorant of the goodness and love of God; he falls, but he repents. The virtuous man might well have taken too much credit for his virtue and become proud about his achievement. He ought to have known better, ought to have been more responsible.

If there is one area where the Lord expects us to act responsibly, it is in our relationships with our fellow-sinners, fellow-members of our parish or community. When was the last time we took our Lord at his word in today's Gospel? The Gospel brings us back to one of the major goals of Lent—purification of the Church, of each member of the Church—not just purification, but wholeness based on mutual love and respect of each member for the others. Jesus tells us that anger and ill-will in any member can threaten or destroy what he wants most for his people, namely, forgiving love that binds up wounds and makes the community an inescapable sign of the presence of God on earth. We can gather from this Gospel how detestable hatred, anger, and ill-will are for Jesus.

We know how he feels about his Father's glorification by all people. But he tells us that, however exalted and necessary worship may be, it has to take second place to reconciliation between members of the community. "If you bring your gift to the altar and there recall that your brother has anything against you, leave your gift at the altar, go first and be reconciled with your brother, and then come and offer your gift." That is incredible! What is even more incredible is that Jesus puts the responsibility on the one who is offended. It must be that the offended one is not entirely without blame. But who it is who initiates or who carries through the reconciliation does not matter; what does matter is reconciliation—a return to wholeness—in the community.

What really concerns Jesus here is that the worship of God by the entire community can be wiped out or spoiled by a single person who refuses reconciliation. But God knows, and we all know, that it happens. We know from personal guilty experience. Judging by this Gospel, our greatest need as Christians is a forgiving heart *and* a heart willing to receive forgiveness. Without that kind of heart, the threat of the First Reading could well be aimed at us: "If a virtuous man turns from the path of virtue to do evil . . . can he do this and still live?"

But Jesus not only talked about the sinner's need for reconciliation with God and his community. He created a special sacrament to help us become (and remain) reconciled. The sacrament of Penance (confession) is now properly called the sacrament of reconciliation. Too many Catholics presently neglect this sacrament. This is tragic, both for them and for the Christian community. Lent is *the* time of the year for a thorough, honest confession. We ought to prepare for it as much as we prepare for and look forward to our Easter entrance into the death and resurrection of Jesus. But we don't have to wait that long. The sooner, the better. Lent will mean so much more to us.

"Lord, deliver me from my distress. See my hardship and my poverty, and pardon all my sins" *(Entrance Antiphon).*

"I trust in the Lord; my soul trusts in his word" *(Responsorial Psalm).*

"By my life, I do not wish the sinner to die, says the Lord, but to turn to me and live" *(Communion Antiphon).*

230 SATURDAY OF THE FIRST WEEK OF LENT

READING I **Deut 26:16-19**
GOSPEL **Matt 5:43-48**

Reading I: Moses reminds his people of the covenant God has made with them and again states the conditions for their part in the covenant.

Gospel: Jesus lays down the law of the new covenant, which he will establish as a fulfillment of the old. The law is love for others, including enemies.

The theme of today's liturgy is law, but not just any kind of law, as we shall see. In Reading I Moses tells his people: "This day the Lord, your God, commands you to observe these statutes and decrees. Be careful, then, to observe them with all your heart and with all your soul." To which we respond: "Happy are they who follow the law of the Lord." Obeying the laws of a nation don't generally make people happy. What's so special about obeying the Law of the Lord? "The law of the Lord is perfect, reviving the soul; his commandments are the wisdom of the simple" (Entrance Antiphon).

The Law of the Lord rests on the single crucial fact of God's having chosen the Jewish people as his very own. He made an agreement, a covenant, with them. He will be their God, he will watch over them, guide and protect them, provided they fulfill their part in the agreement. Their part essentially is freely and lovingly to acknowledge God's Lordship over them; it is to accept his love; it is to trust in him. "Today you are making this agreement with the Lord: he is to be your God and you are to walk in his ways and observe his statutes, commandments and decrees, and to hearken to his voice."

God never intended the covenant to be a burden on his people. He *chose* this people out of all the nations of the world to be his very own, as he often tells them, and that choice was made simply because he loved them. He himself compared the covenant to marriage between a man and a woman. Marriage implies mutual respect, mutual obligations, and above all mutual love. Marriage cannot be static. If it does not evolve into deeper and deeper love and trust, it deteriorates and falls apart. Both parties have to be faithful to the obligations they freely take upon themselves. And that is what this Law of the Lord is all about.

We Christians believe that the Old Testament people of God has evolved into the Church, the Body of Christ, his spouse. At the Last Supper Jesus said: "This cup . . . is the new covenant in my blood" (Luke 22:29). We as a people and as individual members are still responsible for fulfilling our part in the covenant. But we, like the Old Testament people of God, can and do grow careless. The marriage "cools off," as it were. It needs renewal, it needs a "marriage encounter" with our God. Lent is an extended "married couples' retreat" for us and him.

At the Last Supper, Jesus not only established this new covenant between God and us. He also gave us a new law for it, "a new commandment": that we love one another. Yesterday he told us how much we need forgiving hearts. Today he gets tough: "My command to you is: love your enemies, pray for your persecutors. . . . If you love those who love you, what merit is there in that?" And he ends with the command that may seem impossible to fulfill: "You must be perfected as your heavenly Father is perfect."

Fulfilling Jesus' command is what our Christian life — and above all, Lent — is all about. It is a progressive process of cooperating with God in his will to make us a perfect spouse for himself. We can fast, give alms, pray day and night, but it is all a waste of time unless we at least try to fulfill this new commandment of the Lord. The ideal Jesus sets before us is not just tolerance of those who do not like us or whom we do not like. Too often tolerance comes close to mindless indifference, which is the exact opposite of love.

The Opening Prayer tells us so much about our life as members of Christ's Bride, the Church: "Eternal Father, turn our hearts to you. By seeking your kingdom and loving one another, may we become a people who worship you in spirit and truth." Life with

God, like any marriage, has to be worked at. Love is hard, it is a lifetime task that is never finished. Nor will Christ's Bride, the Church, be the perfect bride till the end of time. We can be sure our God will do his part. It is only when we do all in our power to love and forgive that he will take over and love in us, with our hearts; and then we will be perfected as our heavenly Father is perfect.

* * *

"Happy are they who follow the law of the Lord" *(Responsorial Psalm)*.

"My command to you is: love your enemies, pray for your persecutors" *(Gospel)*.

"Be perfect, as your heavenly Father is perfect, says the Lord" *(Communion Antiphon)*.

25 SECOND SUNDAY OF LENT Cycle A

READING I Gen 12:1-4   **READING II** 2 Tim 1:8-10
GOSPEL Matt 17:1-9

Reading I: God calls Abram to leave his land and his old life and go forth into a new land and start a new nation. Abram believes God and goes off into an unknown future.

Reading II: As God called Abram into a new life, so now does he call us to a new life of grace won for us by Christ.

Gospel: Matthew describes the Transfiguration of Jesus.

Last Sunday we found out about the obstacles that might ruin Lent for us, namely, the temptations to vainglory and to want to be like God. Today we learn about the true goal of Lent, our own transformation into Christ.

In the Gospels the Transfiguration of Jesus follows his own prediction of his Passion and death. Supposedly, it was to comfort the apostles and help them understand something about that terrifying event. We can hardly blame them if the attempt was only partially successful. We are used to the Transfiguration. They were not.

It had never happened before. Their understanding came only by hindsight. We should be able to do better.

In thinking about the Transfiguration, we are accustomed to concentrate on the glorious vision of Jesus' divinity shining through his humanity, and we see it primarily as a proof of his divinity. As we shall see, there is something more to it. The dazzling sight first delights the apostles and causes Peter to cry out: "Lord, how good it is for us to be here!" And he wanted to build three booths, he wanted to stay forever. He was fascinated and delighted. His was a perfectly natural human reaction to the desirability of God and the foretaste of heaven that the sight provides. But then they hear the voice of the Father coming from the ancient symbol of God's presence, the overshadowing bright cloud: "This is my beloved Son on whom my favor rests. Listen to him." They fall on their faces in awe and holy terror — the second natural reaction to the experience and vision of divinity, rising from the consciousness of their own sinful unworthiness to be in the presence of the All-Holy One.

But the voice of the Father is significant, not primarily to show how humans ought to respond to the presence of the divine or to give the apostles (and us) proof of Jesus' divinity. The Father's words provide us with an insight into what he has in store for Jesus. The Father proclaims: "This is my beloved Son on whom my favor rests. Listen to him." — almost the identical words the Father spoke at the baptism of Jesus in the Jordan. What is significant is that both times the Father is quoting from one of the Servant Songs of the prophet Isaiah, which foretell the coming Passion and death of the Messiah.

The reason why the Church shows us this glorious image of the Transfiguration of Christ is not only to give us a preview of the resurrection but to point out to us the ultimate effect that our own Lenten life, above all our ongoing conversion to Jesus, is supposed to accomplish in us. We are to be transformed more and more into him so that his features, his love, his compassion may transfigure us. "My heart has prompted me to seek your face; I seek it, Lord; do not hide from me" (Entrance Antiphon).

And that takes us back up the mountain. Jesus touches the fear-stricken apostles and says, "Get up! Do not be afraid." They get up, leave behind their taste of heaven, and follow him down the mountain, down into life again. They enter into the future, not knowing what that future will contain for their beloved Master and for them. They must be filled with apprehension about that future because of his predictions, but they are ready to go with him. They strike out into the unknown. They are true sons of Abraham.

But what about Abraham? There has to be some mysterious connection between Abraham and the Transfiguration of Jesus and us. Is it that Lent for us is as much a journey of faith as God's calling Abraham to leave his old country and way of life to launch out into a new life at age seventy-five? What is certain is that God does call us out of our old way of life, with all its weaknesses, even its imagined security. He calls us to give our life over into his hands as Abraham did.

The experience of Abraham and of the apostles is at the heart of Christianity. "We learn from Abraham (and the apostles) that faithfulness does not mean holding onto something. . . . It consists in courageously saying yes to that Someone who invites us always to move on, to grow in his dream for us" (Barry McGrory: Novalis Homiletic Service, Ottawa, March–April 1979). Every time we give up anything, especially the security of a home, we die a little. But we die in order to rise again and live.

Life must go on. It must be lived now . . . in a creative way. Abraham did not know the future any more than we do. He left that in God's hands. So must we. One of life's most necessary lessons for us is to know how to let go. Life is full of choices, transitions, leave-takings. But none will be too difficult if, like Abraham, like Jesus, like the apostles, we give our lives over to him who says to us, "You are my beloved children on whom my favor rests." And there is Jesus' hand on our shoulder and his voice, "Get up and do not be afraid."

Paul tells us in Reading II: "Bear your share of the hardships which the gospel entails. God has saved us and has called us to a holy life." That call to a holy life, that goal, is what this life of ours is all about. It is surely what Lent is all about. "Lord, let your mercy be upon us as we place our trust in you. Our soul waits on the Lord. He is our help and our shield; Lord, let your love rest on us, as our hope has rested in you" (Responsorial Psalm).

* * *

"My heart has prompted me to seek your face; I seek it, Lord; do not hide from me" *(Entrance Antiphon).*

"Lord, let your mercy be upon us, as we place our trust in you" *(Responsorial Psalm).*

"This is my beloved Son on whom my favor rests. Listen to him" *(Gospel).*

READING I   Gen 22:1-2, 9, 10-13, 15-18   READING II   Rom 8:31-34
GOSPEL   Mark 9:2-10

Reading I: God asks Abraham to offer in sacrifice his beloved son Isaac, and Abraham is ready to obey when the Lord stops him.

Reading II: St. Paul tells us that God did not spare his own Son but handed him over to death for the sake of all of us.

Gospel: The account of the Transfiguration according to Mark is similar to that given by Matthew.

The customary interpretation of the Transfiguration of Jesus as a preparation of the apostles for the coming trial of their faith when they would witness the death of Jesus is legitimate. It is also appropriate to see it as a vivid demonstration of what Lent is supposed to do for us, namely, transform us more and more into Christ — make us new creatures through our sharing in Christ's death and resurrection. All that is fine. But the juxtaposition of this Gospel with the sacrifice of Abraham places it into a new light, and Paul in Reading II puts the meaning in specific terms.

Abraham is surely one of the most remarkable and admirable persons who ever lived. From this distance we cannot possibly imagine his agony and anguish when the Lord commands, "Take your son Isaac, your only one, whom you love, and go to the land of Moriah. There you shall offer him up as a holocaust on a height that I will point out to you." Isaac, we recall, is the "miracle-child" whom God had promised Abraham in his old age. And it is now that same God who makes this gruesome demand! That's part of Abraham's agony. His whole life has been an unfolding act of faith in and love for this God. And now God asks this of him! It is a request that calls into question God's own promises to Abraham — that in him all the nations of the world would be blessed. But now he contradicts himself. This is not like him. This makes God into a kind of ogre, and that, I believe, may well be the heart of Abraham's agony.

But he does not flinch or rebell. He hopes and trusts against hope, and that may well be what real faith is: total trust in the Father, even when that trust seems unreasonable. And when God sees that Abraham is willing to go all the way in believing and trusting, he stops the sacrifice with the significant words: "I know how devoted you are to God, since you did not withhold from me your beloved son." And he blesses Abraham and renews his promises to him.

Beautiful as this first reading is, it is not the whole story and meaning for us today. For that we go to the Gospel. "Jesus took Peter, James and John off by themselves with him and led them up a high mountain. He was transfigured before their eyes." And a voice came from the cloud, saying: "This is my Son, my beloved. Listen to him." These words practically reproduce the prophecy of one of the Servant Songs of the prophet Isaiah, which foretell the Passion and death of the Servant of Yahweh who will suffer and die for all humankind. St. Paul sums it up perfectly in Reading II: "God did not spare his own Son but handed him over for the sake of us all." It is good for us to remember that the Transfiguration takes place shortly before Jesus' Passion and death. It is as though the Father were saying: "This is my Son. Take him, crucify him. Maybe then you will love him a little more. Maybe you can love and trust me a little more."

The parallel between Isaac and Jesus is perfect. Both are the well-beloved—and only—sons of their fathers. Both carry the wood on which they are to be slain. Both are innocent. Both are willing to die freely, out of love. What we can only try to imagine is the anguish that rends the hearts of the fathers at the prospect of seeing their sons sacrificed. Parents who lose a child through death, sickness, or drugs have some idea of the feeling of Abraham and the Father almighty.

We usually think of the Father as a kind of impersonal being, so supreme and almighty that he has no feelings or emotions. But can we possibly believe that this handing-over of his Son cost the Father nothing? If God has no emotions or feelings, where do our emotions and feelings come from? Were we not made in his image and likeness? I don't know who wrote: "This is the mystery of the Love of God and the pain of God," but it parallels the opinion of Fr. John J. O'Donnell, S.J.: "The cross points to a God who is involved in the suffering of our world. Our God is not the executioner but the fellow sufferer" (Commonweal, April 9, 1976, 235).

But what is all this to us? The story is told of a sister at the shrine of St. Anne de Beaupré in Quebec. She saw a distraught mother carrying a tiny child, and she went to meet her. The woman had come a great distance with the child, the only one she would ever have, she thought, and now he had an affliction which the doctors said was incurable. The only hope was a miracle, and she had brought the child to St. Anne's shrine to pray for that. The sister accompanied the mother to the shrine.

"As we prayed," the sister said, "I witnessed the struggle and rebellion of this woman refusing to give up her child. Her sorrow was terrible to see. Yet the miracle came. But it came to the mother, not the child. When she left I knew that she had offered the child back to God and had surrendered him as a gift. A few weeks later I received word that the child had died. But the following Christmas there came a card with the picture of a beautiful baby boy whom the mother had called Michael, the same name she had given to the first son. And the mother wrote: 'Now I have a son Michael in heaven and a son Michael to give me joy on earth.'" (Sr. Mary Alban, Novalis Homiletic Service, Ottawa, March–April 1979).

The story well illustrates today's readings. Being a Christian means being willing to offer back to God what is nearest and dearest to us — as Abraham did, as God the Father did, as the woman in the story did. No one, least of all Jesus himself, ever said that being a disciple of Jesus is easy. What is dearest to us may be a human person, a relative, a friend — or it may just be an old way of life, a profession, or just our opinions and prejudices, our own will. Whatever it is that we give back to God makes us victims like Isaac, like Christ, like little Michael. But it also makes us priests like Abraham, like the Father, and like the mother in the story. But the giving enables us to make our own the words of today's Responsorial Psalm:

> O Lord, I am your servant;
> I am your servant, the son of your handmaid;
> You have loosed my bonds.
> To you I will offer a sacrifice of thanksgiving,
> and I will call upon the name of the Lord.

In a word, God the Father, Abraham, the mother of Michael gave up their most precious possession, their sons. But then they received them back in a new existence, a new presence. There is no Easter glory without first traveling the way of the cross.

* * *

"Remember your mercies, Lord, your tenderness from ages past. Do not let our enemies triumph over us; O God, deliver Israel from all her distress" *(Entrance Antiphon).*

"I will walk in the presence of the Lord, in the land of the living" *(Responsorial Psalm).*

"This is my Son, my beloved, in whom is all my delight; listen to him" *(Communion Verse).*

READING I   Gen 15:5-12, 17-18   READING II   Phil 3:17–4:1
GOSPEL   Luke 9:28-36

Reading I: This is an account of the covenant which God established with Abraham and his descendants.

Reading II: St. Paul tells the Philippians (and us) that their citizenship is in heaven; they and we are to continue to stand firm in the Lord.

Gospel: This gives the account of the Transfiguration of the Lord according to Luke.

"Hear, O Lord, the sound of my call. . . . Of you my heart speaks. Your presence, O Lord, I seek. Hide not your face from me" (Responsorial Psalm).

The human heart has no deeper prayer than this. It is a plea for the fullness of peace, love, joy, truth, life that God himself planted in our hearts. Today's Gospel provides us with a hint of how this fullness will some day be granted to us. Peter says: "Lord, how good it is for us to be here." Seeing Jesus transfigured was a taste of heaven for the apostles. They thought: "Let's just settle down and never leave." But Peter is to learn that he has to live and work and become a little more deserving of the ultimate fulfillment of desire, and so do we all.

It is significant that Christ's Transfiguration in each of the synoptic Gospels is introduced by a prediction of his Passion and death. Thus Matthew: "From then on Jesus started to indicate to his disciples that he must go to Jerusalem and suffer greatly there at the hands of the elders . . . and to be put to death, and raised up on the third day" (16:21). This is noteworthy in that the Church chooses the Transfiguration today when we are still close to the beginning of Lent. Her purpose must be to show us what Lent is supposed to do in us and for us as individuals and as a community. *We are to follow Christ along his paschal journey*, along the way of the cross, up to another mountain, Calvary. Lent is supposed to transform us to the end that we can make our own the words of St. Paul: "I have been crucified with Christ, and the life I live now is not my own; Christ is living in me" (Gal 2:20).

The purpose of Lent is to bring Jesus more and more into our consciousness so that we and our daily life will be transfigured. We may not forget that it is our daily life that matters. It is this daily life that is to be transformed more and more by Christ's grace and presence, above all by his love. Especially by his love, for it is love more than anything else that transforms and makes new beings of us.

There is something else in this marvellous event that deserves careful attention. Recall the words: "While he was praying, his face changed in appearance . . . ." Then came the Father's voice: "This is my Son, my Chosen One. Listen to him." It is significant that while Jesus is praying, the Father presents him to us and says: "Listen to him." That command does more than recommend obedience to Jesus' word and example: It is also a clearcut lesson in how we are to pray, in what prayer really is. Prayer is Jesus Christ speaking to us out of the midst of his own praying, his own self-awareness as the Beloved Son, his consciousness of the Father's presence to him and his presence to the Father. *And* it is our listening with ears and hearts, our loving reception of the words he speaks and our responding to the word out of our own self-awareness. The whole theology and methodology of prayer is here taught us by the Father, the one above all who knows what prayer really is or ought to be.

In prayer Jesus is present to us and we are conscious of his presence. It is in and through prayer that Jesus manifests himself to us, speaks to our hearts, loves us, becomes part of our consciousness.

The evangelists use human terminology to describe Christ's Transfiguration. Matthew says: "His face became as dazzling as the sun . . . ." In our daily experience there are times when the sun does not penetrate the clouds, but we know that it is there. So it is with Jesus' transforming presence to us and his saving, loving word. But if we throw up a personal overcast of unconcern, of indifference, disinterest, busyness, he cannot reach and warm our hearts and being; nor can he transform us with his love. But like the sun, he is always there. We know that. But we are so often like the apostles who, St. Luke tells us, were heavy with sleep. So we have to wake up and stay bright so that we can see his glory.

We all have our deep personal concerns. It is impossible always to be thinking about God or even trying to recall what Jesus says to us in the daily Gospels. But I wonder if, despite our daily preoccupations, there cannot be a mentality of presence, of awareness, of openness to God and *his* presence. It would be like two people who are in love. They go about their business and their work. But they are always present to one another, even when they are apart. And they often think of one another. It is this kind of mentality, of awareness, that wipes away the overcast of indifference and unconcern that prevents the sun of God's loving presence from shining into our hearts and lives.

Deep in our hearts we know how much we need that presence. It is what the psalmist had in mind in giving us that magnificent Responsorial Psalm: "Hear, O Lord, the sound of my call . . . of you my heart speaks; you my glance seeks. Your presence, O Lord, I seek. Hide not your face from me."

When we realize that the God of all love is so present to us, that he loves each of us personally, no matter how sinful we are or think we are, then all of life becomes new, fresh, creative, exciting. *That* God loves us that way—personally, lavishly, unsparingly, even foolishly, is what the Transfiguration of Jesus tells us. It's what Lent is all about; it's what our Christian faith is all about.

Yes, Lord, Peter was right. "Master, how good it is for us to be here," to be present to and with you as you are present to and with us! "God our Father, help us to hear your Son. Enlighten us with your word, that we may find the way to your glory" (Opening Prayer).

* * *

"Remember your mercies, Lord, your tenderness from ages past" *(Entrance Antiphon)*.

"The Lord is my light and my salvation" *(Responsorial Psalm)*.

"This is my Son, my Chosen One. Listen to him" *(Gospel)*.

231 MONDAY OF THE SECOND WEEK OF LENT

READING I   **Dan 9:4-10**
GOSPEL   **Luke 6:36-38**

Reading I: We hear a national act of sorrow by the people of God for their having violated their covenant and rebelled against God and his commandments.

Gospel: Jesus pleads with his followers for compassion, pardon, and generosity towards all peoples.

"Lord, deal not with us as our sins deserve" (Responsorial Psalm). It is not hard to imagine the Lord smiling at that prayer. If he dealt with us as our sins deserve, we'd all be wiped out. But the main reason why the Lord can smile at our prayer is that he doesn't have to be reminded of our need for mercy. Being merciful is what he is and what he has been doing since people first tried to live without him.

The Lord does want us to be aware of our sins and our need for reconciliation with him, and he wants us to beg for forgiveness: "Remember not against us the iniquities of the past; may your compassion quickly come to us." Awareness of sin, of evil in our hearts and attitudes, is the beginning of the road up the mount of personal transfiguration which we glimpsed yesterday.

Reading I contains a most comprehensive national act of contrition which we can all make our own. It was *the people* who agreed to the covenant God proposed to them through Moses on Mount Sinai, and it was the people who violated it by worshiping false gods. Now it is the people through the prophet Daniel who confess their national guilt: "We have sinned, been wicked and done evil, we have rebelled and departed from your commandments and your laws. . . . We rebelled against you and paid no heed to your command, O Lord, our God, to live by the law you gave us through your servants the prophets."

It's hard to imagine any modern nation making that kind of "confession." A national act of contrition belongs to each person who makes up a nation. The sins of each citizen coalesce into a single gigantic rebellion against God, a national violation of the covenant. This is the case with us, too. We individual Christians seldom realize that our personal sins aren't personal at all: When we sin, we add to the comprehensive guilt of the entire Body of Christ, the Church.

The Gospel brings us some concise directives about the nature of our conversion, above all, about how we are to implement the act of sorrow we have made. "Be compassionate . . . . Do not judge . . . . Do not condemn . . . . Pardon, and you shall be pardoned. Give, and it shall be given to you." Again Jesus reminds us that our relationship with God simply has to involve relationships with our fellow members of the Body of Christ and the nation.

The Opening Prayer sums up the purpose of Lent again; it also brings together the strands of this Mass. We ask God to teach us to "find new life through penance." So the purpose of our self-awareness as sinners is not to make us dwell morbidly on our sinfulness but to teach us to find new life through penance and repentance. Sorrow, contrition, is not an end in itself. It is only a means to that new Easter transfiguration at which we are aiming.

The prayer continues: "Keep us from sin, and help us live by your commandment of love." There's not much point in telling God we are sorry (or even going to confession) unless we will try to become better persons. But we know how weak and vulnerable we are; we know we cannot become better persons by our own power alone; so we plead for help that we may be able to live by God's commandment of love. Only love can make us better persons; only love can make us complete persons. To live by God's commandment of love—that's Christianity, that's the heart of the Easter transfiguration that the Church and Jesus its head wish to accomplish in us.

What is fascinating about this prayer is its recognition of our human condition, our frailty, our inability to do anything by our own power. Sometimes, I think that the smile of God mentioned at the beginning may be a bit sad. He's got the whole world in his hands, with all its peoples. But he made them free and they sin, they refuse his love. But he never gives up hoping in us. Our sighing comes before him, and he has mercy. That's the way it is. That's the way he is.

* * *

"Lord, do not deal with us as our sins deserve" *(Responsorial Psalm).*

"We have sinned, been wicked and done evil; we have rebelled and departed from your commandments and your laws . . . But yours, O Lord, our God, are compassion and forgiveness" *(Reading I).*

"Be merciful as your Father is merciful, says the Lord" *(Communion Antiphon).*

232   TUESDAY OF THE SECOND WEEK OF LENT

READING I   Isa 1:10, 16-20
GOSPEL   Matt 23:1-12

Reading I: God warns us to "cease doing evil; learn to do good," and he assures us that no sin is too great to prevent him from forgiving us.

Gospel: Jesus warns against Pharisaeism—going through the external motions of being religious, the heart being absent.

God answers yesterday's national admission of our sinfulness with a stern warning in today's Reading I: "Wash yourselves clean! Put away your misdeeds from before my eyes; cease doing evil; learn to do good. . . . redress the wronged, hear the orphan's plea, defend the widow."

So the Lord throws the responsibility back on us. Repentance and conversion have to involve more than a mere verbal admission of guilt. Conversion has to manifest itself in our actions — in a new way of life, including a change of attitude toward the poor, orphans, and widows: "Make justice your aim, redress the wronged," he tells us.

Usually the Responsorial Psalm is our human response to God's word to us. Today that pattern is broken and God himself continues his demand for repentance, and he becomes specific. We may mistakenly feel at times that we can smooth over our relationship with God or make up for our sins by some kind of external religious deed. Not so, he tells us. Worship has to spring from loving, longing hearts. It is our human response to God's holiness and goodness. We don't worship in order to win God's favor, but because God is God and we are his children, his creatures who never cease needing to acknowledge his Lordship.

"Why do you recite my statutes, and profess my covenant with your mouths," he asks us. "Though you hate discipline and cast my words behind you? When you do these things, shall I be deaf to it? . . . He that offers praise as a sacrifice glorifies me; to him I will show the saving power of God."

The warning against going through the external motions of worship with no backing from loving hearts continues in the Gospel. What Jesus does is to use the Pharisees and scribes as object lessons to us about how *not* to be religious. Since they are supposedly experts in the interpretation of the Law and the prophets, they ought to know all about and take to heart the divine warnings in today's First Reading from Isaiah, to say nothing about Psalm 50's lesson on the nature of true worship.

But they are object lessons in what can happen to "professional religious people," who easily become prone either to distort God's word for their own advantage or who use it as a weapon against members of the people of God whom they despise. It is one of the most ancient of vices, one which is as common among modern Christians as it was among Jesus' contemporaries. They remove God from the observance of God's own regulations — laws intended by him to aid his people to reach full human development — and then use their own outward observance of the Law as a club against others.

Jesus ends his warning to the Pharisees (and us) with the best Lenten advice we have had so far: "The greatest among you will be the one who serves the rest. Whoever exalts himself shall be humbled, and whoever humbles himself shall be exalted." Serving others is the only antidote to whatever degree of Pharisaeism and hypocrisy we might cherish in our thoughts.

But however rough the Lord's words might sound to us today, he does not want us to become overwhelmed by a dismaying consciousness of personal sinfulness. Neither God nor the Church wants us to feel wretched and defeatist about our sins. "Rid yourselves of all your sins, Yes," he tells us in the Gospel Verse. But he continues: "And make a new heart and a new spirit." And the best ingredient for that new heart and new spirit is our God's own never-to-be-retracted assurance: "Though your sins be like scarlet, they may become white as snow; though they be crimson red, they may become white as wool" (Reading I).

After that we can only cry out: "I will tell all your marvellous works. I will rejoice and be glad in you, and sing to your name, Most High" (Communion Antiphon).

* * *

"Wash yourselves clean! Put away your misdeeds from before my eyes; cease to do evil, learn to do good" *(Reading I)*.

"To the upright I will show the saving power of God" *(Responsorial Psalm)*.

"Whoever exalts himself shall be humbled, but whoever humbles himself shall be exalted" *(Gospel)*.

READING I   Jer 18:18-20
GOSPEL   Matt 20:17-28

Reading I: We are told of a plot to destroy Jeremiah, and we hear his prayer to the Lord for deliverance.

Gospel: Jesus predicts his Passion and death, and two of his disciples scheme for privileged places in his kingdom.

"Do not abandon me, Lord. My God, do not go away from me! Hurry to help me, Lord, my Savior" (Entrance Antiphon). This cry belongs to Jesus in his Passion; it belongs to Jeremiah in his. We can certainly make it our own in whatever passion we are all experiencing. Try saying the prayer now. That the Church is an excellent psychologist is marvellously indicated in her choice of readings for these Lenten Masses. Usually the Friday Lenten liturgy gives a preview of the Good Friday tragedy. This week we'll have two previews.

Today's is very realistic. Jeremiah's enemies say: "Let us contrive a plot against Jeremiah. . . . let us destroy him by his own tongue." This is precisely what Jesus' enemies will say and do when the time for his Passion arrives. And Jeremiah's reaction to the antagonism of his enemies is close in spirit to Christ's prayer in the Garden of Gethsemane the night before his death: "Heed me, O Lord, and listen to what my adversaries say. Must good be repaid with evil that they should dig a pit to take my life?"

The Responsorial Psalm continues and adds details to the Passion preview. It actually provides the words that Jesus will use as he hangs on the cross and dies: "Into your hands I commend my spirit." Again, "I hear the whispers of the crowd, that frighten me from every side, as they consult together against me, plotting to take my life." You would almost think that the psalmist was eavesdropping on Jesus as he prayed in the garden, especially in the final words of today's psalm: "But my trust is in you, O Lord; I say, 'You are my God.' In your hands is my destiny; rescue me from the clutches of my enemies and my persecuters." Again, try praying this psalm yourself.

The Gospel situates us close to the end of Jesus' life. His years of preaching, healing, training the apostles are almost over. It is time to inform his followers: "We are going up to Jerusalem now. There the Son of Man will be handed over to the chief priests and scribes, who will condemn him to death. They will turn him over to the Gentiles, to be made sport of and flogged and crucified. But the third day he will be raised up."

If we wish, we can be properly shocked and scandalized at the lack of understanding of the apostles and the incredible ambition that James and John reveal. It is easy for us now at this distance in time to second-guess the apostles and even the Pharisees. But let us not forget: The Church presents these readings and prayers to us, not to make us feel superior to the apostles but to place us in the presence of grace, in the presence of a Savior whose love and suffering for us knew no bounds. And she wants us to respond to that presence with a genuine desire and determination to be converted to Christ with all our being.

It is for us to determine how far we have to go, how much need we have for conversion. And it is good to be reminded again that conversion is more than a change of mind, of heart, of values — important as that change is to true conversion. It is mainly a matter of *growing up in Christ* and in our faith, of becoming that whole "divine-human" being Christ calls us to be.

It is obvious that the apostles needed that kind of conversion. But we also need to remember that they were working at it only three short years or less. What are the years of our lives? How many Lents have we endured? What is the present status of our continuing, life-long conversion? Maybe that's too difficult and sweeping a question to answer. Maybe we could give some kind of evaluation if we would simply apply the standard that Jesus himself gives us in today's Gospel: "Anyone among you who aspires to greatness must serve the rest, and whoever wants to rank first among you, must serve the needs of all. Such is the case with the Son of Man who has come, not to be served by others but to serve, to give his life as a ransom for many." What grade would we give ourselves if we took that test?

* * *

"Do not abandon me, Lord. My God, do not go away from me! Hurry to help me, Lord, my Savior" (Entrance Antiphon).

"I am the light of the world, says the Lord: he who follows me will have the light of life" (Gospel Verse).

"The Son of Man did not come to be served, but to serve, and to give his life as a ransom for many" (Communion Antiphon).

READING I Jer 17:5-10
GOSPEL Luke 16:19-31

Reading I: Jeremiah presents the contrast between the person who trusts in himself rather than in God and the one who places his trust in the Lord.

Gospel: We hear the story of the rich man who is punished in hell on account of his indifference to the beggar lying at his gate.

"Happy are those of blameless life, who follow the law of the Lord" (Communion Antiphon). It's hard to argue with that principle, but hearing the ideal of a blameless life and achieving it are two different things. The problem is this wayward heart of ours, this being that we are and know ourselves to be. God puts these words in the mouth of the prophet Jeremiah: "More tortuous than all else is the human heart, beyond remedy; who can understand it?" Another translation is even more graphic: "The heart is deceitful above all things, and desperately corrupt; who can understand it?"

The answer, of course, is that the heart is *not* beyond remedy, and if no one else can understand the human heart, God can: "I, the Lord, alone probe the mind and test the heart." It is tempting and not at all difficult for me to see the Lord's grim insight into human corruption verified in a lot of people I know or hear about. "How is it possible for him (her) to be so mean?" Then comes Lent with the inspired insight: "It's *me* he is talking about!" Oh, to be sure, I haven't done anything that would earn me a vacation in jail, but what about all those other corrupting temptations I give in to: envy, backbiting, gossiping, hatred, anger, selfishness, the desire for revenge. . . . But why go on? The Lord knows more about me than I do; it is he who tests my heart.

It seems that for God the deadliest wrong I can do to myself is to refuse to remember who God is and who I am. "Cursed is the man who trusts in human beings, who seeks his strength in flesh, whose heart turns away from the Lord." I am sure that the Lord is stating a fact, not actually pronouncing a curse on anyone. The fact is that when I turn my heart away from the Lord, I become like one cursed, I become like a barren bush in the desert that stands in lava waste, a salt and empty earth.

Is this the condition I prefer to the one which the Lord obviously desires for me? "Blessed is the man who trusts in the Lord, whose hope is the Lord. He is like a tree planted beside the waters. . . . that bears fruit." A thousand times, NO! Your words, Lord, not only convict me, they lift me up, they make me see how desperately I need the conversion you hold out to me this Lent. "Test me, O God, and know my thoughts; see whether I step in the wrong path, and guide me along the everlasting way" (Entrance Antiphon).

The First Reading states *in words* the truth about the vulnerability of these poor hearts of ours. The Gospel *dramatizes* at least one kind of corruption that can destroy a person. The rich man's heart has turned completely away from the Lord. Consequently, he indulges himself greedily in fine food. But his worst sin seems to be his *complete indifference* to the poor man lying in rags and starving at his gate. (Again, who was it who said that the opposite of love is not hatred but indifference?)

The drama unfolds and we are not surprised at the outcome. The rich man reaps the reward of his indifference to the poor man, of his having turned away from God. The poor man trusted in the Lord; he is like a tree planted near running water that yields its fruit in due season (Reading I). But the final scene of this drama is the one that Jesus most wants us to make our own. The rich man wants the Lord to send a warning to his brothers, lest they meet his sad fate. Jesus has Abraham responding: "If they do not listen to Moses and the prophets, they will not be convinced even if one should rise from the dead."

So that's how much the Lord thinks of Moses and the prophets, the divine words of Scripture! He obviously expects that word to convert us, to do for us what a person returned from death could not do. But it is not just a question of hearing the word, but of allowing it to take root in our hearts. "Happy are they who have kept the word with a generous heart, and yield a harvest through perseverance" (Gospel Verse). May we all look forward to that harvest of new, recreated hearts at Easter! "God of love, bring us back to you. Send your Spirit to make us strong in faith and active in good works" (Opening Prayer), especially the good work of caring for the poor, of awareness of their presence at the gates of our lives.

* * *

"God of love, bring us back to you. Send your Spirit to make us strong in faith" *(Opening Prayer)*.

"Happy are they who hope in the Lord" *(Responsorial Psalm)*.

"Happy are those of blameless life, who follow the law of the Lord" *(Communion Antiphon)*.

READING I **Gen 37:3-4, 12-13, 17-28**
GOSPEL **Matt 21:33-43, 45-46**

Reading I: We hear the story of Joseph, hated by his brothers and sold as a slave into Egypt for twenty pieces of silver.

Gospel: Jesus relates the parable of the tenants of a vineyard who abuse the owner's messengers, and when the owner sends his son, they kill him: a prophecy of how Jesus will be treated.

Old Testament prophets and men of God foretold the future in words and by what they were and what they did. The story of Joseph is familiar and dear to anyone who has studied the Old Testament. It ought to be dear to every Christian, for Joseph is a perfect fore-type of Jesus. Like Jesus he is sold for some pieces of silver. He becomes a slave in Egypt, but eventually he turns out to be the savior of his people. His life is one of the high points in the history of God's deeds on behalf of his Chosen People.

There is another resemblance that merits some of our attention. The author of Genesis tells us that Israel (Jacob) loved Joseph best of all his sons, and when this fact became evident to his brothers, "They hated him so much that they would not even greet him." There is something prophetic in Jacob's words to Joseph: "Your brothers are tending our flocks at Shechem. Get ready; I will send you to them." Isn't there some resemblance here to John's words in his Gospel: "God loved us and sent his Son to take away our sins" (Communion Antiphon)?

Jesus' words today contain a warning and a prophecy: He tells his enemies a parable that is so graphic that he doesn't have to explain it to them. They recognize themselves in the tenants who kill the owner's very own son, "the one who will inherit everything." And they are terribly offended by Jesus' remark: "I tell you, the kingdom of God will be taken away from you and given to a nation that will yield a rich harvest." He may well have intended this warning as a final plea to his enemies to understand and be converted to him. He wants to love them, but they turn back his love. They will come to a bad end.

It is just a little too easy for us now to read or hear both of these tragic accounts and to judge and condemn the villains. That is definitely not what the Church, and certainly not what Jesus, wants. Instead, "Remember the marvels the Lord has done" (Responsorial Psalm). That's what Jesus wants us to do. Christ's hope and desire is that if we remember what he has done and continues to do for us, we might possibly be overcome by love and be converted. Remembering is a terribly important element in our lives. Try to imagine what life would be like without being able to remember what loved ones have done for us. Try to remember what our religion would be like if we lost all power to remember what Jesus has done for us (and still continues to do). Religion would lose its soul. It would become a mere external formality.

But remembering is not enough. What we need now, this Lent, is not just to remember what Jesus has done for us but to open our hearts to the love that inspired all that he did. This kind of remembering is a very special grace that we are incapable of acquiring by simple human will power. And so we pray: "Merciful Father, may our acts of penance bring us your forgiveness, open our hearts to your love, and prepare us for the coming feast of the resurrection" (Opening Prayer).

So, why not try to remember the ways in which we in our past have made our own the very faults of the brothers of Joseph and of the Pharisees who plotted to do away with Jesus? That kind of remembering is good for the process of repentance we are engaged in. But we don't dwell with those memories; we use them as a springboard to a deeper, more repentant love.

Four weeks from today will be Good Friday, the day when we will remember the suffering and death of Jesus and get all sentimental over it. We've probably had a lot of Good Fridays in our lives and have done a lot of remembering . . . and then gone back to our old habits and ways. So maybe we need more than just remembering. We need to take to heart the desire of Jesus in the Gospel that we become responsible for the vineyard and deliver to the owner his share of the produce. The only produce the Lord is interested in is a Christianized world and from us workers a love for him and for one another ripening into holiness. And so we pray: "God of mercy, prepare us to celebrate these mysteries. Help us to live the love they proclaim" (Prayer over the Gifts).

* * *

"Remember the marvels the Lord has done" (Responsorial Psalm).

"God loved the world so much, he gave us his only Son, that all who believe in him might have eternal life" (Gospel Verse).

READING I   **Micah 7:14-15, 18-20**
GOSPEL   **Luke 15:1-3, 11-32**

Reading I: We see a vision of God who forgives sins, removes guilt, and delights in clemency and compassion.

Gospel: Jesus tells the parable of the Prodigal Son. It is the story of our life as sinners, whom God never gives up on.

"The Lord is kind and merciful. Bless the Lord, O my soul" (Responsorial Psalm). That verse summarizes both readings and gives the reaction we ought to have to the merciful forgiveness of our God. "Not according to our sins does he deal with us, nor does he requite us according to our crimes. For as the heavens are high above the earth, so surpassing is his kindness toward those who fear him." "The Lord delights in clemency," Micah tells us. He casts into the depths of the sea all our sins (Reading I).

But if we want to know who God is and how he actually does delight in clemency, there is no better way of finding out than the Gospel of the prodigal son. And if we want to know who the young son is who wants to try his wings, look in the mirror (we can do the same thing if we want to know the identity of the older son). There are times in our lives when we readily exchange identities from one son to the other, depending on the degree of awareness of sin in our lives or of the artificial holiness that so often results from our own prideful accomplishments.

The young son is thoughtless, he loves risks, he lusts for food, drink, and unlawful sex. Essentially, he is very immature. It is only when he has exhausted the collectivity of his unholy desires that he realizes the futility of trying to satisfy the hunger of his heart with fleeting satisfaction, comes to his senses, and decides to return home to his father.

The motive for his "conversion" is not all that noble. He's hungry, his money and friends are gone. But give him credit; he picks up and goes back, which is more than many modern prodigals do. His father has been waiting for him, runs to meet him, and doesn't even give him a chance to make his "act of contrition." We know what happens next—the banquet, the party, the celebration, the singing—all presided over by the smiling, loving, forgiving father who never gave up on his son. I always like to quote the remark of the poet Péguy that it was not the son who wept, but the father. One can wonder if the young man didn't feel a little embarrassed by it all.

The older son is very much a part of the whole story. He makes no secret of his feelings about the celebration. Envy, anger, hurt feelings, resentment — all seek to possess him. The father's response to his outburst is what concerns us: "My son, you are with me always, and everything I have is yours. But we must celebrate and rejoice! This brother of yours was dead, and has come back to life. He was lost and is found." (Those words also give us some idea of how God feels about our confessions.)

There can be no doubt about the Father's love for both sons. But what matters is that the lost one has been found and restored to the family. And the older son, so concerned all his life about his sense of duty, ought to have realized that there are some things even more important than a sense of duty, not least of which is the integrity of the family.

But what about us? Lent would surely be incomplete without to-day's Gospel about the prodigal son — or rather, the prodigal father, the father who loved so prodigally, so outlandishly. I said above that looking into a mirror will tell us the identity of the younger son (or, if you choose, the older one). If we have imitated the younger one in his abandonment of the father, may we now during Lent come to our senses and make his determination our own: "I will break away and return to my father, and say to him, 'Father, I have sinned against God and against you; I no longer deserve to be called your son.'"

To return to the Father, to be converted, to grow up, to come to our senses and realize where true love and joy are to be found — all this is still our Lenten program, as it is also the aim of the Lenten confession we will make or have made. We may still have a long way to go. But one thing we can be sure of: The Father will be waiting for us, and he will be the one who weeps for joy. He, too, will be the one who presides at the party celebrating our return (The party, of course, is the Mass). "As the heavens are high above the earth, so surpassing is his kindness towards us. As far as the east is from the west, so far will he put our transgressions from us. The Lord is kind and merciful. Bless the Lord, O my soul" (Responsorial Psalm)!

* * *

"The Lord is loving and merciful, to anger slow, and full of love; the Lord is kind to all, and compassionate to all his creatures" (*Entrance Antiphon*).

"He redeems your life from destruction, he crowns you with kindness and compassion" *(Responsorial Psalm)*.

"I will rise and go to my Father and tell him: Father, I have sinned against heaven and against you" *(Gospel Verse)*.

28   THIRD SUNDAY OF LENT   Cycle A

READING I Exod 17:3-7   **READING II** Rom 5:1-2, 5-8
GOSPEL John 4:5-42

Reading I: The people grumble because they have no water. At the command of God, Moses strikes a rock and water gushes forth.

Reading II: Paul tells the Romans that God proves his love for us by the fact that, though we are sinners, Christ died for us.

Gospel: John relates the story of Jesus and the Samaritan woman. He reveals his messiahship to her before he does it to the apostles themselves.

To celebrate Lent well, we need frequent reminders that Lent was originally the final period of the early catechumens' preparation for baptism. But we who are already baptized need this preparation as much as the catechumens. That is, we need the understanding of all aspects of baptism, and, above all, we need the conversion to Christ that was not part of our consciousness when we were baptized as infants.

It is not hard to imagine the catechumens' capacity for self-identification with the characters in all our readings today. In Reading I the Israelites demanded water and complained bitterly to Moses about not having it. They are typical examples of people in need of conversion. God had done great things for them in rescuing them from Egyptian slavery. He had been trying by loving deeds to prove how much he cared for them, but they still wanted to know, "Is the Lord in our midst or not?"

What those Israelites really yearned for — but without realizing it — was not just water, but for what the water stands for, what baptism with water accomplishes, namely, union with God and the gratification, not of bodily thirst, but the thirst of the human heart. It should not be hard for us to identify with that same thirst today, even though we have already been baptized.

Water, and much more, is what the Gospel is all about. The marvellous point about this reading is that it is Jesus who asks a human person—a sinful, outcast woman—for a drink of water. He wants more than water; he thirsts for her heart, her love, her personal commitment to him. God's thirst for us is deeper, much more demanding, than our thirst for him.

This Samaritan woman is surely one of the most fascinating characters in the Gospels, and obviously Jesus thinks so, too. He is a Jew, a rabbi. Jews do not speak to Samaritans, and rabbis never converse with women in public, not even with their own wives. Incredibly, he asks her for a drink of water. She is properly shocked: "You are a Jew. How can you ask me, a Samaritan and a woman, for a drink?" Jesus refuses to accept that stereotype. This woman is a *human person* whom he not only respects but grants the most extraordinary revelation given to anyone at this stage of his ministry. With utmost delicacy and psychological insight, he leads her from surface comprehension of his words to the deepest spiritual understanding of who and what he is.

"If only you recognized God's gift," he responds, "and who it is that is asking you for a drink, you would have asked him instead, and he would have given you living water." There is give-and-take between them, till finally he says: "Whoever drinks the water I give him will never be thirsty; no, the water I give shall become a fountain within him, leaping up to provide eternal life." She doesn't understand—she is still on the natural, material, level—but she is fascinated. "Give me this water," she pleads. But she is not quite ready; she has to go to "confession" first. She has to admit what he already knows, that she is a sinner and has given in to other thirsts, that after five husbands, the man she is now living with is not her husband.

That's getting a little uncomfortable for her, so she changes the subject to the liturgy and the different places and ways of Jewish and Samaritan worship. But he will not let her go. He looks into the future (let us hope that he sees us!) and then tells her: "Believe me, woman, an hour is coming when you will worship the Father neither on this mountain nor in Jerusalem. . . . God is Spirit, and those who worship him must worship in Spirit and truth."

Out of love for us, God gives himself to us. The only response he desires of us is a response in the Spirit. Our response, Jesus tells the woman and us, must involve an inner abandon of our whole self to him. The woman's answer to this beautiful lesson in authentic worship brings her close to the fullness of the revelation Jesus is about to give her: "I know there is a Messiah coming. . . . When he comes, he will tell us everything."

Now she is ready, and so is Jesus. "I who speak to you am he!" How absolutely astounding . . . and how wonderful! Here is a person of loose morals, a member of an outcast breed, a Samaritan, a *woman*, and to her he reveals what he does not consider his chosen apostles ready to know—his own true identity! He surely doesn't do things in a conventional way, and the disciples are properly shocked when they return and find him in deep conversation with the woman. If they only knew what he had just told her!

The woman's reaction is natural and spontaneous. The human heart being made aware of infinite goodness and love cannot keep the secret of that revelation and has to rush off to share it. "Come and see someone who told me everything I ever did! Could this not be the Messiah?" she tells the villagers; and giving in to curiosity rather than her credibility, they follow her to Jesus, thus enabling her to become an apostle leading people to Christ before any of the chosen Twelve. Jesus speaks to them and wins them over. They beg him to remain with them and he stays two days. But even he does not rid these chauvinists of their traditional prejudice against women. They tell her: "No longer does our faith depend on your story. We have heard for ourselves, and we know that this really is the Savior of the world."

It's a magnificent episode in Jesus' life—one that tells us more about him than most of the other well-known Gospel incidents. Have we any reason to believe that Jesus is not as attracted to each of us as to her? The fact that we are here, that we are celebrating Lent and looking forward to Easter and the renewal of our baptism, that we are concerned about a deeper, more intimate relationship with him is at least a beginning of the kind of response he desires from us. What today's Preface says about the woman of Samaria has to be true of us: "When he asked the woman of Samaria for water to drink, Christ had already prepared her for the gift of faith. In his thirst to receive her faith he awakened in her heart the fire of your love."

"Give me a drink," he asks us. But really, what he wants of us is what he wanted of her—our hearts and all our love. If we give in to his request, we will simply be responding to his love for us; there will be an exchange: He will give us his heart.

And then will be fulfilled in us the promise of the Entrance Antiphon: "I will prove my holiness through you. I will gather you from the ends of the earth; I will pour clean water on you and wash away all your sins. I will give you a new spirit within you, says the Lord." Then will Paul's promise be fulfilled: "This hope will not leave us disappointed, because the love of God has been poured into our hearts through the Holy Spirit who has been given to us."

* * *

"If today you hear his voice, harden not your hearts" *(Responsorial Psalm)*.

"The love of God has been poured out in our hearts through the Holy Spirit who has been given to us" *(Reading II)*.

"Lord, you are truly the Savior of the world; give me living water, that I may never thirst again" *(Gospel Verse)*.

29   **THIRD SUNDAY OF LENT**   **Cycle B**

READING I   Exod 20:1-20   READING II   1 Cor 1:22-25
GOSPEL   John 2:13-25

Reading I: We hear the list of the commandments that God gave to Moses on Mount Sinai.

Reading II: St. Paul reveals the content of his preaching, namely, Christ crucified.

Gospel: John gives his account of the cleansing of the Temple and how the Jews reacted to this "sign."

"My eyes are ever fixed on the Lord, for he releases my feet from the snare. O look at me and be merciful, for I am wretched and alone" (Entrance Antiphon).

This is a most human cry. There are many times in life when we feel wretched and alone, but if our eyes are ever fixed on the Lord, we are never alone. And having our eyes fixed on the Lord is always one objective of Lent. It is also an excellent description of religion— always to have one's eyes fixed on the Lord in hope, expectation, and longing desire for deeper oneness with him.

More and more, the Lenten readings reveal God's holy efforts to make clear to us the true meaning of Christ, the Church, Christianity, and our Christian life. These readings attempt to clarify and possibly even correct whatever false ideas we might have acquired about God, Christ, and the Church. This certainly is Paul's purpose in today's Reading II.

According to Paul, the Jews desired a Messiah who would obtain for them their national sovereignty and independence. The Greeks wanted a kind of perfect human wisdom that would provide a satisfactory explanation of human beings and give some meaning to life. Paul writes: "We preach Christ crucified, a stumbling block to the Jews, and an absurdity to the Gentiles." For the Jews the Christ Paul preached was an object of revulsion and anger whom they cannot possibly accept, and to the Gentiles Paul's Christ was absolute madness and stupidity. But this Christ is God's own idea. How right was the painter Rouault to depict Christ as a clown, the object of scorn and ridicule. *This* Christ is the power and wisdom of God. And we are coming to know that God's foolishness is wiser than human wisdom and God's weakness is stronger than all human strength.

Does this kind of language sound absurd? Is it possible for God to be foolish, to be weak? If we take offense at such an idea, we simply do not know God. In himself and in Christ he is sheerest common sense and wisdom.

Again, like all the Lenten readings, today's summon us to a re-examination and re-evaluation of our own ideas about Christ, about the Church, about Christianity; and today there is special emphasis on one of the elements of Christianity — the commandments of God. For the Jews the two most sacred institutions were the Law and the Temple. Both were God's own idea. Jesus upheld them. Law is good, it is necessary; without it every human institution is the prey of anarchy and destruction. So, too, the Temple was good. It was the very focal point of Hebrew life and religion. It was the dwelling-place of God's glory. The people saw it as the very antechamber of heaven.

Unfortunately, however, at the time of Jesus some of the rabbis and teachers had perverted the original divine intent and meaning of both the Law and the Temple. They made the Law in particular into an *end*, rather than a *means* for bringing the people closer to God and giving them an opportunity to respond freely and lovingly to God's holy will. In making the rigid, minute observance of the Law the essence of religion, they were guilty of making human effort and success the heart of religion. People saved themselves by their own efforts. They did not need any other savior. They did not need God's foolish generosity in giving them a Christ who would be God's idea of salvation, not theirs.

All his life Jesus contradicted these false ideas and interpretations of the Law, and his efforts brought him the death and resurrection which he himself foretold in today's Gospel. What Jesus actually wanted to do in casting the money changers out of the Temple was to purify the ideas and misunderstandings which his enemies had of the Temple. The death he predicts for himself is to bring the old covenant to an end and inaugurate the new and eternal covenant that will rise out of his sacrifice. "This cup is the new covenant in my blood," he will say at the Last Supper.

Jesus replaces the old covenant and its institutions with a *person*, himself. God in Christ reveals himself, not in the Law and the Temple, but in the scandal of a crucified Messiah. The covenant-God comes to his people in human weakness, vulnerability, and shame.

But what meaning does all this have for us? Today's readings tell us that seeking security in the observance of law, making the heart of religion to consist primarily in obedience to law without love as the essential motivation (even the sacred Ten Commandments of God himself) is to be guilty of the same false misunderstanding of religion that Jesus condemned in the Pharisees.

To be sure, a right understanding of the commandments can be a great help towards our conversion — which we remember is the chief purpose of Lent. The commandments have been called moral imperatives, which means that their purpose is not just to make us avoid evil but to direct our life towards a higher and more positive goal. They constitute a code of behavior for all humankind. But we also need to remind ourselves that just observing laws will not bring about conversion. Jesus tells us what is really needed: "I give you a new commandment: Love one another. Such as my love has been for you, so must your love be for each other" (John 13:14).

Most of us have been taught that the meaning of sin is that it is disobeying a commandment, but in the light of Jesus' new commandment sin is much more than disobeying a commandment or a law. Sin essentially is ignoring the *person* behind the law — God, "who so loved the world that he gave his only Son. . . ." Sin is a rejection, a scorning, of love; it is refusal to enter into the personal love relationship that God extends to us all. When I sin, I turn my back on God and prefer myself to him.

The Word was made flesh and dwells now among us. Jesus gives himself to us and wants to enter ever more and more intimately into these lives of ours. When we allow him entrance, when we look upon him as the Gospels present him to us, we begin to see ourselves in a new perspective, and if we look honestly into our hearts, we might be shocked at the discovery of how little progress we have made in intimacy with Jesus. Christ's goodness, his light, truth and, above all, his overwhelming personal love for each of us convict us of our need for conversion.

It is Jesus who summons us to this conversion, which aims not only at identifying our basic sinful deeds but also our basic sinful hearts so that we can start out in a new direction for our lives. In the light of Christ's holiness and goodness, we have to face up to the truth about ourselves and learn what it is within our hearts that makes us think and speak and act as we do. We simply cannot accept the truth about the Lord, the truth about the Gospel, until we first accept the truth about ourselves. And there is no sacrament like the sacrament of reconciliation that can help us not only accept the truth, but do something about it. This sacrament and the "sacrament" of Lent mean *change* or they mean nothing at all.

The evangelist John tells us that Jesus is well aware of what is in the human heart. When our knowledge of what is in these hearts of ours corresponds with what he knows, then we are ready for his personal healing, the transforming power contained in the Eucharist and in the life-giving, life-changing sacrament of reconciliation.

* * *

"My eyes are ever fixed on the Lord . . . . O look at me and be merciful, for I am wretched and alone" *(Entrance Antiphon)*.

"Lord, you have the words of everlasting life" *(Responsorial Psalm)*.

"Lord, in sharing this sacrament may we be brought together in unity and peace" *(Prayer After Communion)*.

READING I Exod 3:1-8, 13-15   **READING II** 1 Cor 10:1-6, 10-12
GOSPEL   Luke 13:1-9

Reading I: We are present at the famous scene when God speaks to Moses out of the burning bush and tells him to lead the captive Jews to the Promised Land.

Reading II: St. Paul uses incidents from the history of the Jews to warn the Christians (and us) not to become overconfident in our spiritual striving.

Gospel: Jesus likewise uses the history of his people to preach the need to reform.

"My eyes are ever fixed on the Lord, for he releases my feet from the snare. O look at me and be merciful, for I am wretched and alone" (Entrance Antiphon).

That's a good prayer, especially for those of us who suffer and agonize mentally or physically. It is also a program for Lent: a plea for help, as well as the best way to assure that help will be coming to us, namely, our eyes fixed on the Lord.

"Grow up!" is a normal reaction in anyone who thinks that someone else is acting irresponsibly. Grow up! Act your age! It is not recorded in Scripture that God ever used that expression on his people, but actually it is what he wanted most of them, and now most of us, to do.

We have been meditating on our need to be converted ever since Lent began, and we have explored many different insights into the nature of conversion. To grow up and become responsible, mature human beings and Christians is the most expressive of all. It's not an original idea. Psychiatrists see conversion essentially as growing in a sense of responsibility. For example, Gordon Allport has written that in no region of personality do we find so many residues of childhood as in the religious attitudes of adults. Most of us mature in every other area of life except in our ideas of God, prayer, worship, and the living out of our Christian faith.

Repentance is the first step on our way to fulfillment as a human person. The call to conversion builds on the lack of unity in our lives. It responds to a natural human need, the need for wholeness, the need to put together the scattered pieces of our lives. And the specifically Christian aspect of conversion is being confronted with Jesus in whom the believer sees the breadth and depth of what it means to be a whole human being. In Jesus we see what our own life is called to be.

All the readings today present a challenge to all of us to grow up. In Reading I God breaks into the settled, pleasant, relaxed life of Moses and asks him to go on a mission for him that will change not only Moses' life but the course of history. In verses 9 to 12 (left out of today's reading) Moses puts up all kinds of objections, the main one being his poor self-image, his inability to believe in himself. "Who am I that I should . . . lead the Israelites out of Egypt?" he asks (v. 11). But God will not take no for an answer. He insists on Moses' becoming the instrument of his mercy and compassion: "Go and tell my people: 'The Lord, the God of your fathers, the God of Abraham, the God of Isaac, the God of Jacob, has sent me to you.'"

God's eagerness to save his people will not be denied. The liturgy uses Psalm 103 to respond to God's merciful and divine intent: "The Lord is kind and merciful. . . . Merciful and gracious is the Lord, slow to anger and abounding in kindness. God was merciful and gracious then. He still is to and for us.

In the Second Reading St. Paul uses the subsequent history of the Chosen People to bring home a very necessary lesson to his community at Corinth (as well as to our community, our parish). For Paul the Israelites' passing through the Red Sea is a type of baptism. The manna they eat in the desert is a type of the Eucharist. Paul is telling the Corinthians that the Israelites had something like our sacraments: "They all drank from the spiritual rock that was following them, and the rock was Christ."

But the Israelites rebelled against God and had to suffer the consequences. Paul is writing to people who have the Christian sacraments. But despite the Lord's outpouring of grace, strength, and spiritual food, the Corinthians are torn by divisions and petty strife. Paul warns them: "All these things happened to them [the Israelites] as a warning, and it is written down to be a lesson for us who are living at the end of the age." Actually, what Paul was saying was simply, "GROW UP!"

Although perhaps not immediately evident, the message of Jesus in the Gospel is much the same as that of Paul. He asks: "Do you think that these Galileans [on whom the tower fell] were the greatest sinners in Galilee just because they suffered this? By no means! But I tell you, you will all come to the same end unless you reform." Unless you reform . . . unless you grow up. The call of Jesus, the call of Paul, of the Church for repentance and conversion is meant for all of us. There is never a time in our lives when the need for repentance and conversion ceases.

Jesus does not want us to wonder and worry about when we shall meet our judge. Our problem is: How do we respond *now* to the good news that in God's eyes we count, we matter, just as much as the Israelites mattered to him so long ago? To the good news that life is worthwhile, that it is purposeful?

God has chosen us to be responsible members of his Church. That means that there is a divine purpose for each of us; that is why he is constantly summoning us to conversion. Each of us without exception needs to do better, to think better, pray better, share better, care better, love better, live better and more maturely than when we were younger. Each of us needs to become more creative, more productive instruments of God's redemptive love. Reform your lives, Jesus insists. Accept the new life and above all the new responsibility for your faith that I am offering you now and during the rest of this Lent.

Who does not need to become more and more Christlike? Of course, it is much easier to call for others to reform their lives than to see the need for reform in our own. We have to remember that the persons who reform themselves have already contributed to the reform of their neighbors. That's a lesson that may be very useful to many parents.

So often we become like the barren fig tree in the Gospel. We bear no fruit or if we do, it is bitter and dried up. But Jesus never gives up on us. He never ceases to plead with the Father to have patience with us: "Leave the tree another year while I hoe around it and manure it; then perhaps it will bear fruit." Christ's patient mercy might well be the most important point in the Gospel. The Gospel contains grim warnings but also merciful love. But how many "next years" are there? When will we run out of time?

Jesus is talking to us today about growing up, about allowing him to convert us. Lent is the time for Christ to fertilize us, to hoe the hard ground around our hearts so that he can bring us to new life, to a rebirth in the Easter dying and a rising with him. Can we refuse the invitation?

* * *

"My eyes are ever fixed on the Lord, for he releases my feet from the snare. O look at me and be merciful for I am wretched and alone" (*Entrance Antiphon*).

"Bless the Lord, O my soul; and all my being, bless his holy name" (*Responsorial Psalm*).

"Repent, says the Lord, the kingdom of heaven is at hand" (*Gospel Verse*).

READING I   2 Kgs 5:1-15
GOSPEL   Luke 4:24-30

Reading I: Naaman, a Syrian leper, is cured by bathing three times in the
Jordan River.

Gospel: Jesus returns to his home town Nazareth, but he is rejected by
his old friends, who want to kill him.

"My soul is longing and pining for the courts of the Lord; my heart
and my flesh sing for joy to the living God" (Entrance Antiphon).
We can all make that sentiment our own just by saying the words
with feeling. The liturgy never allows us to forget that these Lenten
Masses not only remind us of our need to grow in our faith, to be
converted, but they recall that the daily texts were the final period
of instruction for the catechumens preparing for their Holy Saturday
baptism. Today we share the thirst for the living waters of baptism
that sprang from the hearts of those early candidates, and in so doing we are brought face-to-face with our own spiritual condition
now. We have to ask ourselves, for example, how much that basic
thirst for God is part of our life—whether or not our having been
baptized makes any difference in our life.

The army commander Naaman was a pagan. He did not thirst
for God, or if he did, he didn't realize it. All he wanted was a cure
for his leprosy, he wanted to be whole again. (But isn't that what
baptism is all about for us Christians—the healing of our wounded
being, being made whole in the Lord? And may we not say the same
about the sacrament of reconciliation?) But there is something else
in the story of Naaman that is good for us to reflect upon. He expected healing from a man, the prophet Elisha: "I thought that he
[the prophet] would surely come out and stand there to invoke the
Lord his God, and would move his hand over the spot, and thus cure
the leprosy." And he is terribly let down at the prophet's command
to wash in the Jordan.

He decides to go home, but his servants restrain him: "If the
prophet had told you to do something extraordinary, would you not
have done it?" The saving lesson for him (and for us) is that God
works best and most effectively through ordinary people and places
(like the little servant girl, the servants, the Jordan) because ultimately it is God who does the cleansing, the making whole. Human
beings are only his instruments. Naaman obeys, is cleansed of his
leprosy, and then comes to faith: "Now I know that there is no God
in all the earth, except in Israel."

That's the way he felt about being made whole by the waters of the Jordan. Do we come close to feeling the same way about our being made whole in baptism? Do reminders like Naaman intensify the thirst for God that is deep in our hearts, often without our being aware of it? "Athirst is my soul for God, the living God. When shall I go and behold the face of God (Responsorial Psalm)?

In the Gospel Jesus is in trouble. The people of Nazareth are irked by his statement: "There were many lepers in Israel in the time of Elisha the prophet; yet not one was cured except Naaman the Syrian." His old friends and relatives reject him. He had come home to his own, but they refused to accept him. It must have been one of the saddest moments of his life. Apparently, they had become too used to him to see him for what he really was, God's own Son (that may well happen to us, too). That was one problem. The other was that they could not believe in him because they could not believe in themselves. But at the root of all the difficulty here is that apparently they had lost that thirst for the living God that alone can bring divine gratification for all human aspirations.

The Gospels do not tell us if Jesus ever returned to his home town. But we do know that he returns to the town of our hearts year after year, day after day. He thirsts for us. May we never cease to pray: "My soul is thirsting for the living God, when shall I see him face-to-face" (Responsorial Psalm)? May we make the Gospel Verse our very own: "I hope in the Lord, I trust in his word, with him there is mercy and fullness of redemption."

* * *

"Lord, forgive our sins and bring us together in unity and peace" *(Prayer After Communion).*

READING I Dan 3:25, 34-43
GOSPEL Matt 18:21-35

Reading I: We share Azariah's poignant prayer for forgiveness, following upon the admission of guilt for having forsaken the Lord God.

Gospel: With the parable of the unforgiving servant, Jesus drives home the lesson that we must forgive one another again and again.

One essential element in our Lenten conversion is willingness to forgive those who have hurt us; it is willingness to be forgiven by those whom we have offended; it is *reconciliation* with our God, our neighbor, and ourselves.

"Irrational" is about the only word that can describe the central figure in the Gospel—the official whose king forgave him an enormous debt but who refused to have mercy on a fellow official who owed him only "a mere fraction of what he himself owed." We ask ourselves how he could be so cruel (and so stupid), and immediately the answer comes: "You've done the same thing yourself again and again." The master hands the unforgiving servant over to the torturers "until he paid back all that he owed." How frightening the final conclusion: "My heavenly Father will treat you in exactly the same way unless each of you forgives his brother from his heart!"

"With all your heart turn to me, for I am tender and compassionate" (Gospel Verse). Reading I gives us a lovely example of obedience to that divine suggestion. Azariah speaks for his people (and we can make his sentiments our own): "We are reduced, O Lord, beyond any other nation, brought low everywhere in the world because of our sins." Awareness of one's sinfulness is the first step towards reconciliation. But more than awareness is required. We can pray with Azariah again: "But with contrite heart and humble spirit let us be received . . . . So let our sacrifice be in your presence today, as we follow you unreservedly . . . . And now we follow you with our whole heart . . . . Deliver us by your wonders, and bring glory to your name, O Lord."

One of our problems in arriving at any kind of lasting reconciliation with our God is our human weakness and the seeming inevitability of sinning. But that's a defeatist attitude that needs to be overcome. Sin is indeed present to us and in us. But what Jesus (and the Church) is telling us today and all through Lent is that there is something greater than sin present to us: It is forgiveness, it is divine love. "Lord, you call us to your service and continue your saving work among us. May your love never abandon us" (Opening Prayer).

That's a prayer we can be sure will be answered. God's love never abandons those who experience a true need for it.

But we have to come back to the obligations that God's forgiveness imposes upon us. Above all, we have to be aware that we are all members of the Body of Christ, the Church, and that receiving God's forgiveness for our failings demands of us that we pass it on.

And may we never forget that forgiveness *has to be received and accepted*, whether it is from God or from one whom we have offended. And then, even more basic, is the need we all have to forgive ourselves. If God thinks we are deserving of forgiveness, we have no choice but to imitate him and forgive ourselves for whatever injuries we do to ourselves by our sins, our failures. (Is there any need to be reminded that the sacrament of reconciliation is the best way for us to accept and receive forgiveness?) Nor may we forget that forgiveness of sins by God is more than having our sins covered over with a poultice that leaves the wound intact. God's forgiveness is healing, it is restoration to life and vigor, it is being re-empowered with the ability to live and act out of love for God and one another.

So today's Mass might well be one of the most important of the Lenten season, both for individual Christians and for the entire Church and each community within the Church. Nothing we do during Lent, no amount of self-denial or positive works like increased prayer or attendance at Mass will avail us anything unless we see reconciliation as the goal of it all — reconciliation with God, with one another, with ourselves, and with our world. "With all your heart turn to me," says Jesus, "for I am tender and compassionate."

* * *

"And now we follow you with our whole heart, we fear you and we pray to you" *(Reading I).*

"Remember that your compassion, O Lord, and your kindness are from of old" *(Responsorial Psalm).*

READING I   Deut 4:1, 5-9
GOSPEL   Matt 5:17-19

Reading I: Moses pleads with his people to observe the Law that the Lord God has given them and to remember all the good deeds God has done for them.

Gospel: Jesus tells us that he has not come to abolish the old Law but to fulfill it.

Today's liturgy leads us to reflect again on the right place of law in the process of our Lenten life: "I have not come to abolish the law and the prophets. I have come, not to abolish them, but to fulfill them."

The process of conversion — our chief Lenten concern — is both human and divine. It is divine in the sense that it is God who directs it and who actually accomplishes the inner transformation of our hearts (which is what conversion is all about). It is human in the sense that it needs some guidance, some path to follow, lest it go off in all directions, ultimately ending up just where it was at the beginning. So, at this stage of Lent some reflection on the place of law in the Christian life is very essential.

Jesus says: "Do not think that I have come to abolish the law and the prophets. . . ." That's a very significant statement. Because of his frequent condemnation of the Pharisees, some of his followers then (and especially now) may have thought that the Law was no longer necessary for his followers. But his main aim was to correct the false understanding of the Law that persisted among his enemies. For them the Law was not "the friend of man" (W. H. Auden). It was not the loving expression of the Father's will for his children. It was rather a threatening sanction they held over the people to scare them into being good. They made the Law into an end in itself, maybe even equal in importance to God himself. Or again, they saw their loyal and meticulous fulfillment of the Law as a means of putting God in debt to them, in some cases actually thinking they could buy salvation by their own efforts.

If they were right, then Jesus as Savior was unnecessary: They saved themselves by observing all the rules and regulations. All this is behind Jesus' words today: "Do not think that I have come to abolish the law. . . ." No, not to abolish the Law but to provide us with the right idea of it — that idea which Moses voices today, telling us that observing the statutes of God "will give evidence of your wisdom and intelligence to the nations." Moses makes clear that

God's laws and statutes are the expression, not only of his love but of his divine wisdom, his closeness to his people, his deep interest in their daily lives. God doesn't need our obedience to law; we do, in order to be wise and holy and whole. In this sense law can be a lift carrying us up to God.

Moses goes on to give some terribly important advice that is as valid today as it was then: "Be earnestly on your guard not to forget the things which your eyes have seen, not let them slip from your memory as long as you live." Remembering all that God has done for us, all that Jesus has done, his personal involvement in our lives, the countless times he has forgiven us and has been an "occasion of grace" to us—remembering all this ought to stir up within us that hunger for God, that desire for his love, that is all he needs to bring us to the conversion he so very much desires for us during this Lent.

Jesus said that he had come not to abolish the Law, but *to fulfill it*. Not that there was anything incomplete or imperfect about the old Law. Jesus meant rather to bring out its deep meaning as the loving expression of his Father's will. He fulfills the will of his Father when he accepts humiliation and death in obedience to that will out of love for us. Morality for us is responsiveness to God's goodness and love—a responsiveness that we can live out by lovingly following God's law, his will. And conversion for us follows the same path. "Lord, you will show me the path of life and fill me with joy of your presence." "He is our God, and we are the people he shepherds, the flock he guides" (Responsorial Psalm).

* * *

"Lord, direct my steps as you have promised, and let no evil hold me in its power" *(Entrance Antiphon)*.

"Your words, Lord, are spirit and life; you have the message of eternal life" *(Gospel Verse)*.

"Lord, you will show me the path of life and fill me with joy in your presence" *(Communion Antiphon)*.

READING I   Jer 7:23-28
GOSPEL   Luke 11:14-23

Reading I: Jeremiah relates the sad story of the disobedience of God's Chosen People to his Law.

Gospel: Jesus rejects the accusation that he expels demons by Beelzebul and concludes that "he who is not with me is against me."

These daily Lenten Masses were originally composed primarily for the final instruction of those to be baptized at the Easter Vigil, the catechumens. They had been converted months before but were eagerly looking forward to their baptism on Holy Saturday night. The readings and prayers of the Masses were intended to sharpen their thirst for God, to increase their desire for total loving union with Jesus and the Church which baptism would bring. Some readings (like those of today) were also intended as warnings to be prepared for a possible loss of their first fervor, once they were baptized and had experienced the rigors of the Christian life.

We who are already baptized can find these daily liturgies just as pertinent to our lives and to the program of ongoing, never-ending conversion to which Jesus never ceases to summon us: "With all your heart turn to me, for I am tender and compassionate" (Gospel Verse). The Gospel is as much for us now as it was originally for the catechumens: It presents us with the fatal choice: "The one who is not with me is against me. The one who does not gather with me scatters." It is *either-or*, not *both-and*, and no compromising. Jesus demands total, all-out commitment to him and to his way of life:

> Oh, that today you would hear his voice:
> "Harden not your hearts as at Meribah,
>   as in the day of Massah in the desert,
> Where your fathers tempted me;
>   they tested me though they had seen my works" (Responsorial Psalm).

Being realistic, the Church makes use of every argument to confirm and advance us in our conversion. Reading I is a brief summary of the history of the Chosen People. "Thus says the Lord: This is what I commanded my people: listen to my voice; then I will be your God and you shall be my people. Walk in all the ways that I command you, so that you may prosper. But they obeyed not, nor did they pay heed. They walked in the hardness of their evil hearts and turned their backs, not their faces, to me." It was a people, a nation, that failed, a people whose love had grown cold.

The lament is for us as individuals as much as for the people, the

Church. The reading takes us back over the past year, over our past life. It confronts us with the hardness of our own hearts, with our refusal to heed God's word and take correction, with our infidelity, our neglect of the sacrament of reconciliation.

It is a pessimistic, frightening account that Jeremiah relates, and we ask: Is apostasy on such a universal scale all that inevitable? Not if God can help it. We may give up on ourselves. He never gives up on us. "I am the Savior of all people, says the Lord. Whatever their troubles, I will answer their cry, and I will always be their Lord" (Entrance Antiphon). He does more than encourage us; he actually pleads: "With all your heart turn to me, for I am tender and compassionate" (Gospel Verse). Think of that as Jesus' personal invitation to go to confession.

That kind of assurance and prayer demands a response, and again our God himself supplies it: "Come, let us sing joyfully to the Lord; let us acclaim the Rock of our salvation; let us greet him with thanksgiving; let us joyfully sing praise to him; Come, let us bow down in worship; let us kneel before the Lord who made us. For he is our God, and we are the people he shepherds, the flock he guides" (Responsorial Psalm).

* * *

"I am the Savior of all the people, says the Lord. Whatever their troubles, I will answer their cry, and I will always be their Lord" *(Entrance Antiphon).*

"Thus says the Lord: This is what I commanded my people: Listen to my voice; then I will be your God and you shall be my people" *(Reading I).*

"If today you hear his voice, harden not your hearts" *(Responsorial Psalm).*

READING I .Hos 14:2-10
GOSPEL   Mark 12:28-34

Reading I: Hosea pleads to the people to return to the Lord, who will heal their wounds and recreate them as new beings.

Gospel: When asked which is the greatest commandment, Jesus simply repeats what every Jew knows: It is total love for God and love of neighbor as oneself.

Today's liturgy not only tells us how much our God wants us to repent. It again reveals the true meaning of repentance as a return to God, allowing him to reconcile us with him, above all, allowing him to love us as much as he wants. "Return, O Israel, to the Lord, your God; you have collapsed through your guilt. . . . Say to him, 'Forgive all iniquity, and receive what is good, that we may render as offerings the bullocks from our stalls.'" Well, what God wants from us is not any kind of animal. He wants our hearts, our desire for healing, our willingness to allow him to love us.

Reading I is an object lesson in how God responds to the simplest expression of sorrow: "I will heal their defection, I will love them freely, for my wrath is turned away from them." The prophet goes on to describe the flowering of new life that will result from our return to our God: "I will be like the dew for Israel; he shall blossom like the lily. . . . His splendor will be like the olive tree. . . . Because of me you bear fruit."

So, conversion, reconciliation with our God, is not just the forgiveness of sins, the erasing of one's sinful past. It is new and more abundant life, incomparably more gratifying than any kind of worldly good. The psalmist knows how to put it in words: "Lord, there is no god to compare with you; you are great and do wonderful things, you are the only God" (Entrance Antiphon).

But this new, abundant life which results from conversion is a fragile creation that needs to be cared for, like any precious possession. It needs *loving care;* and so we pray today: "Merciful Father, fill our hearts with *your love* and keep us faithful to the gospel of Christ. Give us the grace to rise above our human weakness." And God knows, better than we, the extent of that weakness!

The readings say nothing about being converted to laws and rules: just to love — total, all-out, all-comprehensive love for the Lord our God. "He is the One, there is no other than he." "To love him with all our heart, with all our thought and with all our strength, and to love our neighbor as ourselves is worth more than any burnt offering or sacrifice." Jesus has nothing but praise for this comment by the scribe.

But we always need reminders about what love really consists in. Certainly, it is not romantic, emotional attraction to another person or even to God the Father or Jesus his Son. The whole person is involved in loving—mind, heart, emotions, will. Our mind tells us what the loved one is worth, how much the loved one has loved us and given self to us. The heart and emotions direct the manner and degree of our responding to love. The will helps us determine to live for the beloved, to make the beloved the center of our lives. This is how we must love God. It is also how we must try and want to love our neighbor, including those who are not especially lovable or who reject our love.

Lent is the time for returning to this kind of love; for purifying and perfecting our love.

We can never be satisfied with our loving, either for God or for a beloved spouse or friend. We all know from experience how delicate and fragile love is, how easily it can be wounded and even destroyed. The only love that is not fragile or in danger of destruction is God's forgiving love for each of us.

We know, too, that the kind of love the Lord desires for us and from us is not possible for us to generate by our own strength alone. Only he can impart it, and so we pray in the Communion Prayer: "Lord, fill us with the power of your love. As we share in this eucharist, may we come to know fully the redemption we have received." It's a prayer our God is certain to answer—if only we want it answered, if only we are willing to allow ourselves to be loved.

* * *

"Lord, there is no god to compare with you; you are great and do wonderful things, you are the only God" (Entrance Antiphon).

"Repent, says the Lord, the kingdom of heaven is at hand" (Gospel Verse).

"To love God with all your heart, and your neighbor as yourself, is a greater thing than all the temple sacrifices" (Communion Antiphon).

READING I   Hos 6:1-6
GOSPEL   Luke 18:9-14

Reading I: God pleads with his people to return to him: "It is love I desire, not sacrifice, and knowledge of God rather than holocausts."

Gospel: Luke relates the famous contrast between the self-righteous Pharisee and the humble publican who realizes he is a sinner and begs God for mercy.

We have now lived through three weeks of Lent and have undoubtedly noticed that just about every one of these daily Masses has a different theme and proposes a fresh ideal. But all the themes coalesce into the single overriding one of Lent as a time of renewal—renewal of the Church, renewal of each of us, her members. The true nature of the renewal is spelled out for us in today's prayers and readings: It is nothing less than the death and resurrection of Jesus becoming operative in our lives.

The Opening Prayer gives us that insight: "Lord, make this lenten observance of the suffering, death and resurrection of Christ, bring us to the full joy of Easter." The word "observance" here obviously is not just "looking at"; it is entering into, making that death and resurrection our very own as we experience the pain, sorrow, and worry of daily living. The *observance* so understood is also the theme of today's reading from Hosea:

> Come, let us return to the Lord,
> For it is he who has rent, but he will heal us;
>   he has struck us, but he will bind our wounds.
> He will revive us after two days;
>   on the third day he will raise us up,
>   to live in his presence.
> Let us know, let us strive to know the Lord;
>   as certain as the dawn is coming . . . .
> He will come to us like the rain,
>   like spring rain that waters the earth.

So our goal is Easter, it is rising with Christ to a new and renewed life, and we'll be celebrating that glorious happening three weeks from tonight. But we may not forget the three weeks of penance still remaining. There is no Easter without Good Friday, no "living in the presence of the Lord" without first having died to self and to sin through our Lenten penitential life. But both Hosea and Jesus remind us of the "dangers" of penance without the absolutely essential component, love. "It is love I desire, not sacrifice, and knowledge of God rather than holocausts."

The Pharisee in the Gospel ought to have known Hosea, but that knowledge isn't evident in Jesus' description of him. His good deeds are so present to him that he rattles them off as from a cassette recorder. "I, I, I . . . I did all this. What do you think of that, Lord? I'm different, certainly from that tax collector there." The Pharisee was a very holy man, at least according to outward appearances. But he had a bad memory. He forgot the key meaning of religion as phrased by the psalmist: "It is steadfast love, not sacrifice, that God desires" (Responsorial Psalm). It was that steadfast love that his self-exalting boastfulness had smothered, if it had ever been there at all.

The tax collector, on the other hand, didn't need the Pharisee to tell him his sins. He stood at a distance, "not even daring to raise his eyes to heaven. All he did was beat his breast and say, 'O God, be merciful to me, a sinner.'" Jesus' judgment is emphatic: "Believe me, this man went home from the temple justified but the other did not. For everyone who exalts himself shall be humbled while he who humbles himself shall be exalted." What does "humbling himself" mean if not that the poor man was terribly aware of his total helplessness without God, and therefore he was totally open to him and his forgiving love?

So we are back again to where we were at the beginning of Lent — face-to-face with ourselves and our sinfulness. Our penitential acts (remember them — prayer, fasting, almsgiving?) can be very useful in helping us keep in mind the tax collector's plea, "O God, be merciful to me, a sinner." But may we not forget what is even more important than the penitential acts: "It is steadfast love, not sacrifice, that God desires." It could be that lack of "steadfast love" is what was wrong with our confessions up to now.

It is that kind of spirit and only that, that will enable us to make the rest of this observance of the suffering, death, and resurrection of Jesus result in the full joy of Easter. Then we will be able to cry out with joy: "Bless the Lord, my soul, and remember all his kindnesses, for he pardons all my faults" (Opening Antiphon).

* * *

"It is steadfast love, not sacrifice, that God desires" (Responsorial Psalm).

"Everyone who exalts himself shall be humbled while he who humbles himself shall be exalted" (Gospel).

READING I   1 Sam 16:2, 6-7, 10-13   READING II   Eph 5:8-14
GOSPEL   John 9:1-41

Reading I: We hear the account of the Lord's choice of David to be anointed king of the Chosen People.

Reading II: Paul pleads with his people to live as children of light.

Gospel: A man born blind receives his sight after Jesus anoints his eyes with mud and sends him to be washed in the pool of Siloam.

"Rejoice, Jerusalem! Be glad for her, you who love her; rejoice with her, you who mourned for her, and you will find contentment at her consoling breasts" (Entrance Antiphon). There are many reasons for rejoicing today as we pass the halfway mark of Lent. Because we are human and not particularly wild about doing penance, it is natural for us to rejoice that the penitential season of Lent is nearing its end. But because we are Christians and hopefully closer in mind and heart to Jesus than we were before, it is also natural for us to rejoice at our nearness to his triumphal resurrection . . . and our personal sharing in it.

It's not hard to imagine the rejoicing of the early catechumens today, as the night of their baptismal dying and rising with Jesus looms so prominently before them. And the texts of today's Mass must certainly have stirred up their longing for Christ, even as they do ours now. Each of the readings contains a direct reference to baptism, and each is meant for us as well as originally for the catechumens.

Reading I tells of the dramatic manner in which the Lord, through Samuel, chooses David as the king of his people and the ancestor of the future Messiah. The Lord's words and actions here are significant. He says: "Not as man sees does God see, because man sees the appearance, but the Lord looks into the heart." (We may well wonder what he sees when he looks into our hearts now.)

Then comes the dramatic and unexpected choice of the boy David and his being anointed with oil, "and from that day on, the spirit of the Lord rushed upon David." But isn't this exactly what baptism does for us? We too were anointed with oil; we received the onrush of the Holy Spirit, and now we are no longer what we were. We are new beings, with a new vocation and destiny, just as David was.

"The Lord is my shepherd; there is nothing I shall want" (Responsorial Psalm). The Lord watches over us as a shepherd watches over his sheep. As a shepherd knows his sheep, so does the

Lord know us and call each of us by name. He loves us, we belong to him. The guidance, the nourishment, the repose, the protection a shepherd gives to his sheep—all this the Lord now provides for us. Praise him! "Only goodness and kindness shall follow me all the days of my life; and I shall dwell in the house of the Lord for years to come."

The drama of the Gospel has been and is now being played out in the lives of each of us. Even though we are already baptized, Christ continues to confront us with himself—his person, his example, his teaching and guidance. If we are really willing to open up our hearts to him, he will light up the darkest corners of those hearts in all their stark reality. In the light of his presence the truth about us is exposed. Jesus brings us to a crisis situation where we have to examine ourselves and determine whether or not we are really on our way to full discipleship with him or just dragging our feet.

Like the nameless man in the Gospel, we were all born blind. Then we were washed in the waters of baptism, and we received our sight. We were able to see Jesus, able to glimpse some direction for our lives. Unfortunately, most of us have not lived out our baptism along the lines of dying to sin in order to live unto God. And that is why we need this Lenten renewal year after year. The fact of our having once been baptized either as a child or as an adult does not remove from us the struggle between the forces of light and those of darkness within us and on all sides around us.

But back to the blind man. Only gradually does he come to see who and what Jesus is for him. He is obviously very fascinated by him. He moves slowly from seeing him as an extraordinary healer to seeing him as a prophet sent by God, and then finally, face-to-face with Jesus, he gratefully acknowledges Jesus as the Son of God, the Son of man. Compared to the Pharisees, the blind man illustrates a process of increasing insight into the identity of Jesus as opposed to their condition of progressive hardening blindness and hatred.

Lent, especially what remains of it, has the purpose of exposing to ourselves the truth about ourselves . . . but not in a threatening way. Jesus—in all his goodness, his lovableness, his desirability—confronts us. He makes us take a good look into our hearts, makes us ask in all honesty: "Is Christ *really* the light of my life? Do Gospel values shape my day-to-day existence? Do I concoct compromises with his teaching? How serious am I about caring for the unfortunate, about forgiving my neighbor, about giving up my resentments? How genuine is my alleged love for him?

"As long as I am in the world," Jesus says to us today, "I am the light of the world." He has risen, he is still in the world, in our midst. A few years ago one of the most popular songs young people were enjoying was "You Light Up My Life." It was a love-song intended for a beloved friend. But like so many popular songs, it contained some deep spiritual truth. We can sing those words to Jesus now. Is there anyone who lights up our lives more than he does? "I am the light of the world, says the Lord: the one who follows me will have the light of life" (Gospel Verse).

We may not know the words of the song, but we can make up our own, starting with the first verse. I suggest that we do this between now and Holy Saturday night when we will follow the lighted Easter candle, representing Christ, risen from the dead, and know that in our hearts the light represented by the candle is now the light of our lives. Even though we walk in dark valleys after that, we will fear no evil; for we will know that Jesus is the Light of our lives, he is at our side, he goes before us into our lives with his rod and staff to give us courage.

* * *

"Let us hasten toward Easter with the eagerness of faith and love" (*Opening Prayer*).

"The Lord is my shepherd; I shall not want. In verdant pastures he gives me repose" (*Responsorial Psalm*).

"The Lord rubbed my eyes; I went away and washed; then I could see, and I believed in God" (*Communion Antiphon*).

READING I   2 Chr 36:14-17, 19-23   READING II   Eph 2:4-10
GOSPEL   John 3:14-21

Reading I: This reading tells of God's people's infidelity and their exile in Babylon.

Reading II: St. Paul gives the theology of redemption: "It is owing to his favor that salvation is yours through faith. This is not your own doing; it is God's gift."

Gospel: Jesus explains to Nicodemus that he is to be lifted up so that all who believe in him may have eternal life.

Three weeks from today we will celebrate Easter. In the Opening Prayer we plead: "Let us hasten towards Easter with the eagerness of faith and love." That's easier said than done, primarily because so much remains to be done in our conversion journey to greater intimacy with Christ.

The readings today review the past and look into the future. They also look into our own hearts. Reading I locates the Jews in exile in Babylon—displaced, unhappy persons, one and all. It isn't hard to imagine their pain at being in captivity and their longing to return to their homeland, and it is pleasant to rejoice with them when they hear of their promised deliverance through the kindness of King Cyrus. Their sinful past rises to memory as they suffered in exile: "By the streams of Babylon we sat and wept as we remembered Zion. . . . Let my tongue be silenced if I ever forget you [Jerusalem]."

But who are these exiles now? The candidates for baptism should not have any difficulty identifying with them, but the real identification is with those of us who have exiled ourselves from Christ by our sinful alienation, in whatever form it assumes. Making our own the ideas and sentiments of the Jewish exiles in Babylon will be a good indication to our God that we have come to our senses and are eager and anxious for our repatriation, our homecoming, our reconciliation with Jesus and the Church through our Easter confession and the renewal of our baptism during the Easter Vigil.

Conversion, or reconversion, to Christ involves not only a turning away from a sinful past but also turning away from false ideas about the true nature of our Christian faith. One of the commonest temptations of Christians of any persuasion is to want to control or manipulate God for their own advantage. That temptation arises from our fallen nature; it goes back at least as far as our first parents. It is *the* original sin. We want to be in charge, even of our own salvation. We want to work out our salvation by things we do for God. We want to put God in debt to us. This is precisely what God condemned in the Pharisees. They didn't need a Messiah-Savior; they could assure their own salvation just by their minute observance of the Law. And we often think the same way: "If I am good, if I do good deeds, then God will reward me with all kinds of favors here and with salvation in the end."

Both Jesus and St. Paul tell us it just isn't so. Paul says in the Second Reading: "It is owing to his [God's] favor that salvation is yours through faith. This is not your doing, it is God's gift; neither is it a reward for anything you have accomplished, so let no one pride himself on it." And Jesus is equally emphatic: "Just as Moses lifted up the serpent in the desert, so must the Son of Man be lifted up, that all who believe may have eternal life in him. Yes, God so loved the world that he gave his only Son, that whoever believes in him may not die but may have eternal life" (Gospel).

We have to be very clear in our minds about this. Our Lenten fasting, self-denial in whatever form, works of mercy, suffering, and religious exercises — all this does not cause or bring about God's grace and salvation. On the contrary, if we are doing all kinds of praiseworthy, holy deeds, it is because God's grace is active in us. By our good deeds we simply respond to God's mercy and love for us. I don't know who it was that phrased this basic truth so perfectly: "God doesn't love us because we are good; we are good because God loves us. We don't have to change for God to love us; God loves us and therefore we can change; we don't have to crank out virtues to earn God's love; he loves us first and thus we have the strength and desire to be virtuous." In a word, our good works are a *response* to God's love, not the cause of it.

> "Father, you enlighten all who come into the world.
> Fill our hearts with the light of your gospel,
> that our thoughts may please you,
> and our love be sincere" (Prayer After Communion).

If we can overcome our desire to be self-achievers in matters of religion during this Lent, we will have come a long way towards that permanent conversion willed for us by Christ Jesus. Why is it so hard to believe that we do not have to prove our worth in the eyes of God by our accomplishments? That need is a sure sign of our immaturity as human persons, above all as Christians. The truth is that we are worthwhile in God's sight, not because of what we accomplish but because he loves us and has created us in his own image and because Jesus died for us. We have to believe in our own worth in the eyes of God. So why don't we relax like a little child and allow God to love and care for us?

Today is Laetare Sunday, as the Entrance Antiphon indicates: "Rejoice, Jerusalem! Be glad for her, you who love her; rejoice with her, you who mourned for her, and you will find contentment at her consoling breasts." Jerusalem, our Mother; Jerusalem, our Church; Jerusalem, the home of God's people. Rejoice, because your children are on their way home, home to a true and better understanding of the part that God's enduring love and forgiveness plays in their lives.

It is a Sunday of rejoicing because it recalls to us that we are God's works of art, created by his grace, not by our personal efforts. Let our tongues be silenced if we ever forget that God so loved the world and each and every one of us—sinners and saints alike—so much that he gave up his only Son, that all who believe in him might have eternal life.

* * *

"By the streams of Babylon we sat and wept when we remembered Zion. . . . Let my tongue be silenced, if I ever forget you" (*Responsorial Psalm*).

"I repeat, it is owing to his favor that salvation is yours through faith. This is not your own doing, it is God's gift" (*Reading II*).

"God so loved the world that he gave his only Son, that whoever believes in him may not die but may have eternal life" (*Gospel*).

READING I   Josh 5:9, 10-12
GOSPEL   Luke 15:1-3, 11-32   READING II   2 Cor 5:17-21

Reading I: This is an account of the first Passover celebrated by the Israelites in the Promised Land. The manna ceases and they eat the fruit of the land.

Reading II: St. Paul begs: "I implore you, in Christ's name: be reconciled to God."

Gospel: St. Luke relates one of the most beautiful of Jesus' parables, that of the prodigal son: "This brother was dead, and has come back to life."

Of all the Gospel incidents, the parable of the prodigal son fits most perfectly into Lent — and into the life of every prospective convert, every Christian. This parable distills and sums up the whole meaning of the Gospel, of the Father as a true father to each of us, indeed, more than a father. The parable tells us more about God, about the real meaning of God, than an entire course in theology. To be sure, we can never exhaust the meaning of God, but in contemplating the father of the prodigal son, we approach as close as is possible to the real nature of God. The parable is told by the one who knew him best, Jesus, his own Son.

The story tells us about ourselves, too — about the vagrant, wandering, vulnerable, wounded human heart that is in us all. We can easily recognize ourselves in that young prodigal. We have all insisted on our independence at some time or other. We have insisted on freedom from the constraints and discipline of home, family, superiors. Above all, we can identify with the prodigal son when we think back only a few weeks to the condition we were in before Lent began. But I'll come back to that.

The father is very modern in his permissiveness. We almost have to ask: "Is this the way God is, too?" It seems so, because he knows that freedom for us is the only way he is going to receive any love from us. The father respects the boy's freedom, his desire to live his own life, even though he knows what will happen if he lets him go off with a pocketful of cash. But both this father and the Father in heaven know that the only way some young people learn is the hard way, the sad, personal experience of using their freedom of choice in a selfish way. And God our Father knows that there can be no true love for him unless his children are free not to love.

St. Luke does not go into detail about the young man's subsequent life. Just that "he squandered his money on dissolute living."

You can read the juicy details the unsympathetic older son supplies from his imagination. The essential thing is that the young man finally came to his senses and decided to return home. He even composes his "act of contrition": "Father, I have sinned against God and against you; I no longer am worthy to be called your son." His motive for returning may not have been terribly heroic or supernatural. His money had run out, he was hungry; he had experienced the sad aftertaste of self-defeat. His contrition was at best "imperfect." No matter. The father now takes over.

He has been waiting for the lad. I can see him climbing a nearby hill every day to watch and wait and hope. Finally, his hope is rewarded when he catches sight of the boy in the distance. St. Luke tells us that the father was "deeply moved." "He ran out to meet him, threw his arms around his neck, and kissed him." The poet Péguy makes it more specific: He says it was not the son who cried, but the father. Tears of joy. The boy tries to declare his confession and contrition; the father did not even want to hear it. His beloved son had come home, hoping for reconciliation. There's got to be a celebration, a party. He calls for the finest robe, a ring for the boy's finger, shoes for his feet, and he kills the fatted calf. "Let us eat and celebrate because this son of mine was dead and has come back to life. He was lost and is found."

I repeat: The whole story is about us—about humanity in general and each of us in particular. Maybe our departure from our Father's house has not been so dramatic, nor the results so painful. There are degrees and degrees of alienation. But God our Father takes risks with us, just as the father in the parable did. It's a risk he takes because, despite all our imperfections, he never gives up believing in us and trusting us to come through, if not right away, then eventually. That's why he gives us Lent year after year. It may also be the reason why he gave us the sacrament of reconciliation.

The story of the prodigal is re-enacted in our lives every time we present ourselves to a priest for the sacrament of reconciliation, but it is made present in a very special way during Lent. Lent is the time for the great return, for coming to our senses and saying: "Father, I have sinned against you. I no longer deserve to be called your child."

And the result of this return is more than a simple gesture of reconciliation. We cannot understand this parable fully apart from Paul's teaching in the Second Reading. When the prodigal son returned home and was welcomed back by his father, there was a new relationship between them; the boy was no longer what he was. But what Jesus does for us in our Lenten renewal and conversion, especially in our Lenten confessions, is much deeper and more dramatic. St. Paul puts it this way: "If anyone is in Christ, he is a new creation. The old order has passed away; now all is new! All this has been done by God, who has reconciled us to himself through Christ and has given us the ministry of reconciliation." (With that kind of language, is there any wonder that the sacrament of Penance is now called the sacrament of reconciliation?)

God forgives, he takes us back, he recreates us in the image of Jesus his Son, and then he celebrates our return with a festive banquet. "Let us eat and celebrate, because this son of mine was dead and has come back to life. He was lost and is found." That party, that celebration is the Mass — daily Mass, Sunday Mass, but above all the festive Mass of the Resurrection Holy Saturday night and Easter Sunday. It is at this banquet that the Father says to us as he said to the elder son: "All that I have is yours." It is here that we can all cry out: "Taste and see the goodness of the Lord. I will bless the Lord at all times, his praise shall be ever in my mouth. . . . Look to him that you may be radiant with joy."

Laetare Sunday is for rejoicing, not only for us but for the Father. "Let us hasten toward Easter with the eagerness of faith and love" (Opening Prayer). We could hardly find a more appropriate prayer than that!

* * *

"Taste and see the goodness of the Lord. Look to him that you may be radiant with joy, and your faces may not blush with shame" (Responsorial Psalm).

"If anyone is in Christ, he is a new creation. The old order has passed away; now all is new" (Reading II)!

"My son, you should rejoice, because your brother was dead and has come back to life; he was lost and is found" (Communion Antiphon).

READING I   Isa 65:17-21
GOSPEL   John 4:43-54

Reading I: Isaiah tells of his vision of the "new heavens and the new earth" that God will create at the end of time when there will be no more weeping, nor crying, nor sadness.

Gospel: Jesus heals a sick boy at a distance, simply by a word.

You would have to be a catechumen eagerly looking forward to Easter baptism to appreciate the full measure of joy and desire aroused by Isaiah's vision of new heavens and a new earth: "The things of the past shall not be remembered or come to mind. Instead, there shall always be rejoicing and happiness in what I create . . . . No longer shall the sound of weeping be heard there, or the sound of crying."

What Isaiah is foretelling is the coming of the era of the "messianic times," when the redemption begun by Christ's death and resurrection will have captured and been captured by all humankind. The beginning of those times are not far off for the catechumens.

The Bible does not reveal much about those messianic times when all of creation will be renewed, actually made brand new. And the Christian life being one of faith, it is not necessary for us to know the details. But what we can do is to take comfort in the promise and to hope and yearn for their arrival. St. John, in the Book of Revelation, gives us grounds for that hope. His vision is very detailed:

> Then I saw a new heaven and a new earth; for the first heaven and the first earth had passed away . . . . And I saw the holy city, new Jerusalem, coming down out of heaven from God, prepared as a bride adorned for her husband; and I heard a great voice from the throne saying, "Behold, the dwelling of God is with men. He will dwell with them; he will wipe away every tear from their eyes, and death shall be no more, neither shall there be mourning nor crying nor pain any more, for the former things have passed away" (21:1-4).

We need boosts like that in the midst of Lent, the midst of life. Every convert who has ever been baptized has discovered what the born-Catholic knows by sad experience—that conversion and becoming a new creature in baptism do not automatically dispatch him/her into a painless–sorrowless, deathless world. Pain, sorrow, anxiety—yes, even the possibility of sinning—remain the common lot of every person in the world, baptized or not. What the prospective new Christian can look forward to, however, is the joy of being one with Christ: the joy of knowing that his personal passion and sorrow are an extension of the Passion and death of Jesus . . . and therefore redemptive. And accordingly there will be meaning in life that was not there before.

The Gospel relates a wonderful "sign" worked by Jesus at Capharnaum. He restores a sick boy to health just with a word spoken at a distance from the boy's home. The boy's father had pleaded with Jesus for the boy's health, he trusted in him, and his trust earned the simple assurance: "Return home, your son will live." And his whole household became believers as a result of the sign.

In these incipient messianic times we live in, Jesus continues to heal us, but hardly from a distance. He lives now in his Church, in us, and he acts on us to heal, to nourish, to comfort, and to forgive our sins in and through the sacraments, "the extensions of his humanity," as St. Leo the Great called them. Christ heals especially through the sacrament of reconciliation.

But he heals those only who, like the royal official, experience a great need for him which they are unable to cope with by their own personal strength. "Lord, I put my trust in you; I shall be glad and rejoice in your mercy, because you have seen my affliction" (Entrance Antiphon). That prayer is now ours, and so much the better if we can add to it: "Hear, O Lord, and have pity on me; O Lord, my helper. You changed my mourning into dancing; O Lord, my God, forever will I give you thanks . . . . I will praise you, Lord, for you have rescued me" (Responsorial Psalm).

"This was the second sign that Jesus performed on returning from Judea to Galilee" (Gospel). John's Gospel is "the Gospel of signs." Jesus is the greatest Sign of all. He tells us by his deeds as much as by his words how much we mean to him, how much he loves us. "O Lord, my God, forever will I give you thanks."

* * *

"Lo, I am about to create new heavens and a new earth . . . there shall always be rejoicing and happiness in what I create" (Reading I).

"You changed my mourning into dancing; O Lord, my God, forever will I give you thanks" (Responsorial Psalm).

"Sir, come down before my child dies. . . . Return home. Your son will live" (Gospel).

READING I   Ezek 47:1-9, 12
GOSPEL   John 5:1-3, 5-16

Reading I: Ezechiel describes his vision of water flowing from the Temple growing into a stream that flows into the salt sea which becomes fresh. Fruit trees of every kind grow along the banks of the river.

Gospel: At the Sheep Pool Jesus heals a man who has been waiting thirty-eight years to be plunged into the miraculous waters.

The theme of life-giving water again dominates the readings and texts of today's Mass. "Come to the waters, all who thirst; though you have no money, come and drink with joy" (Entrance Antiphon). The time for the prospective convert's baptism is drawing near. We can imagine the glow of anticipation they experienced when they heard these words. Come to the waters? They can hardly wait! Two years (and more) after their conversion to Christ is a long time to wait for full membership in him and his Church.

We all know, of course, that the water is only a sign pointing to the deep inner effects that the waters of baptism will produce in them. Water brings new growth to parched or desert soil. Reading I puts it so well: "Along both banks of the river, fruit trees of every kind shall grow; their leaves shall not fade, nor their fruit fail. Every month they shall bear fresh fruit, for they shall be watered by the flow from the sanctuary. Their fruit shall serve for food, and their leaves for medicine." Obviously, all these botanical wonders point to the spiritual marvels Jesus will produce in the catechumens at the moment of their baptism. "Come! Behold the deeds of the Lord."

We need to be reminded that we don't have to imagine ourselves as catechumens to share their desire and thirst. Even the waters of baptism cannot quench the thirst for God that he himself planted deep in our hearts. We can and do always long for greater and greater union in love: "All who thirst, come to the waters." The Opening Prayer is not just for catechumens but for us: "Father, may our lenten observance prepare us to embrace the paschal mystery and proclaim your salvation with joyful praise."

To embrace the paschal mystery is to die and rise with Jesus. It is the ultimate glory of every human, baptized or not. If we do not yet experience the fullness of the thirst for God signified by the living waters of baptism, it may well be that our thirst has been dulled by some kind of personal alienation from Christ. Conversion to Christ is ongoing; it never ends. So Jesus appears to us today as he did to the man at the pool of Bethesda, asking, "Do you want to be healed?"

It's a good question. Do we really *want* to be healed? How much healing do we want? This conversion we claim to be working at, is it for real and for how long? We don't have to tell our Lord that we have no one to plunge us into the healing pool. We know where the healing pool is now: It is the sacrament of reconciliation, it is confession, where he heals just as really as he healed the man at the Sheep Pool. The healing pool is also the Eucharist, and certainly, it will be the grace-filled moment of our baptismal renewal Holy Saturday night and Easter.

What the early catechumens longed for, we possess now: baptism and the Eucharist, to say nothing of the sacrament of reconciliation that is always available. We don't even have to wait for Easter to enjoy that. Even now we can begin our free and joyous sailing down the stream whose runlets gladden the city of God, the holy dwelling of the Most High God.

But reconciliation now or later: What we really look forward to and thirst for is our Easter encounter with him who is our Good Shepherd, who says, "I lay down my life for my sheep." He satisfies all our wants and desires and needs. In green pastures he will give us rest, he will lead us along the waters of peace (Communion Antiphon). God is, and always will be, in our midst. Praise him!

* * *

"Come to the waters, all who thirst; though you have no money, come and drink with joy" *(Entrance Antiphon)*.

"The mighty Lord is with us; the God of Jacob is our refuge" *(Responsorial Psalm)*.

READING I   Isa 49:8-15
GOSPEL   John 5:17-30

Reading I: God assures his people that he loves them more than a mother can possibly love her child; he comforts and has mercy always.

Gospel: The growing enmity towards Jesus is based on his claim that God is his Father. He claims that he desires to do his Father's will.

"The Lord has forsaken me; my God has forgotten me" (Reading I). Who is there who has not at some time or other felt like making those words his or her own? Who is there who does not have some kind of cross? Near-despair often threatens to overwhelm an increasing number of Christ's followers. And being reminded of the universality of suffering helps little to comfort the sufferers. What they need is a response to the plea: "I pray to you, O God, for the time of your favor. Lord, in your great love, answer me" (Entrance Antiphon).

It must be kind of hard for the Lord to turn away from such a poignant cry. And he does not. Rather, he reassures us: "In time of favor I answer you, on the day of salvation I help you . . . . Can a mother forget her infant, be without tenderness for the child of her womb? Even should she forget, I will never forget you" (Reading I). Despite all appearances to the contrary, despite all the problems and evils that seem to pile up on us, he never forsakes us, never ceases to love and care for us.

We may have acted badly towards him, and we may even, for all we know, do it again. No matter. Scripture tells us again and again: "The Lord is gracious and merciful, slow to anger and of great kindness. The Lord is good to all and compassionate toward all his works. . . . The Lord lifts up all who are falling down and raises up all who are bowed down. . . . The Lord is near to all who call upon him, to all who call upon him in truth" (Responsorial Psalm).

Some people might become skeptical about such comforting sentiments when mountains of grief seem to be falling on them. But have they, have we, ever given these ideas a chance? Have they sunk into our consciousness? St. John tells us: "God loved the world so much, he gave his only Son, that all who believe in him might have eternal life" (Gospel Verse). "All who believe in him. . . ." That means, all who trust him, who never cease to hold out their hands and hearts to him. Jesus is God's loving forgiveness. He is God's compassionate love and concern for us made flesh. Is he that for us? It could be that the greatest fruit of this Lent for us is to believe at long last how very much God loves us and consequently to allow ourselves to be swept up into that love.

As long as we live we will experience pain and anguish in greater or lesser degree, most of it resulting from the pain and anguish that afflict those dear to us. But Jesus has taken our human flesh on himself, which means being one with us in the flesh. He is one with us also in our pain, worry, and anxiety. The identification is complete. We are not alone, nor is he in his Passion and agony. We are with him as much as he is with us.

This may not be terribly consoling for some. It depends on how much they have permitted bitterness to control their emotions. But the certain knowledge of our being loved to such an extent can fill us with a tremendous sense of what we mean to God, a mighty sense of our own worth. And this might well be what we need most in this world—a sense of our own worth, despite what we might think, despite what anyone else might seem to think. God in Christ loves me that much we can ask? The answer comes to us from today's Gospel Verse: "God so loved the world so much that he gave his only Son. . . ." The world Jesus is talking about is people; it is us; out of love for us he gave his life.

The Lord is indeed near to all who call upon him, to all who call upon him in truth (Responsorial Psalm).

* * *

"I pray to you, O God, for the time of your favor. Lord, in your great love, answer me" *(Entrance Antiphon)*.

"The Lord is gracious and merciful, slow to anger and of great kindness. The Lord is good to all and compassionate toward all his works" *(Responsorial Psalm)*.

"God sent his Son into the world, not to condemn it, but so that the world might be saved through him" *(Communion Antiphon)*.

READING I   Exod 32:7-14
GOSPEL   John 5:31-47

Reading I: Moses pleads with God who wants to punish the people for falling into idolatry, and the Lord relents.

Gospel: John continues the confrontation between Jesus and his enemies who wish to destroy him. Jesus claims to be sent by God and calls on Moses to justify him.

The words "forgetting" and "remembering" are among the most significant in the Bible. *Forgetting* is negative and destructive. *Remembering* is positive and constructive, it can be redemptive. Both words have played an extremely important role in the history both of the Jews and the Christians.

The First Reading relates a typical case of the evil of forgetting. The people of God refuse to remember that God is God, and they are creatures who are totally dependent on him for all that they are and possess. They refuse to remember how he had rescued them from slavery in Egypt, and in this culpable forgetting they become depraved. They create for themselves a god of molten gold, which they worship and acclaim with sacrifices.

The author of Exodus proceeds to depict their true God in a very human manner: He becomes angry and declares his intention to destroy them. But they have a mediator in the person of Moses who pleads for them, who "reasons" with God as though he were human and who finally plays his trump card: "Remember your servants Abraham, Isaac and Israel . . . and your promise to make their descendants as numerous as the stars of the sky and to give them this land as a perpetual heritage." And the Lord does remember (as though he needed to be reminded), and he relents in the punishment he had threatened.

We may well wonder what all this has to do with us here and now. Actually, isn't it our own story, the story of the lives of many of us? We too often refuse to remember who and what we are in the sight of our Creator. We reject his love, just as did the Jews in the desert and the enemies of Jesus whom he confronts in today's Gospel. He says to them: "His voice you have never heard . . . neither do you have his word abiding in your hearts. . . . You do not accept me . . ., and you do not have the love of God in your hearts" (Gospel). This is a terrifying accusation, and we have to search our own hearts to verify if the accusation is true of us.

What are we to do? The only thing we can do is to cry out with the voice and words of the psalmist: "Lord, remember us, for the love you bear your people." We can identify in our hearts the golden calves we have made. We have too often refused to remember all that the Lord has done for us, especially in giving us Jesus as our brother together with his word and his Eucharist as nourishment for our hearts. We have forgotten that he chose us to be his very own people. But you, Lord God, remember the love you have for us, not our crimes!

And the Lord has remembered (as though he ever could forget). He has remembered and we have been trying hard to remember, too, especially during this Lent. Lent is the time of the year par excellence for remembering, for turning back to our God, for re-establishing full and intimate relationship with him.

Lent is the time for taking to heart the recommendation of the Entrance Antiphon: "Let hearts rejoice who search for the Lord. Seek the Lord and his strength, seek always the face of the Lord." Remembering, receiving, seeking—that's what Christianity is all about. Remembering that "man does not live on bread alone (or on anything material, any kind of golden calf), but on every word that comes from the mouth of God" (Gospel Verse). Receiving that word, and above all him for whom it stands, him whom it describes. And then letting that word enkindle in our hearts an inexhaustible, insatiable thirst for God, for more and more of his love which alone can satisfy us.

Remembering and never forgetting. This is our program for the rest of Lent and the rest of our lives. It sums up all religion. With that kind of ideal inspiring us, the Lord's promise to us will be fulfilled: "I will put my law within them, I will write it on their hearts; then I shall be their God, and they will be my people" (Communion Antiphon).

* * *

"Let hearts rejoice who search for the Lord. Seek the Lord and his strength, seek always the face of the Lord" *(Entrance Antiphon).*

"Lord, remember us, for the love you bear your people" *(Responsorial Psalm).*

READING I   Wis 2:1, 12-22
GOSPEL   John 7:1-2; 10:25-30

Reading I: The author of Wisdom gives minute details of a plot to kill a just man simply "because he is obnoxious to us."

Gospel: Aware of the plot to kill him, Jesus nevertheless goes to Jerusalem in secret. In the Temple he again proclaims his divine origin.

Today's Mass anticipates every nuance of feeling, emotion, tragedy, and anguish of Good Friday, only two weeks away. The plot against "the just one" described in Reading I is so detailed, so full of venom and hatred, one might think it came out of a secret meeting of his enemies. "Let us beset the just one, because he is obnoxious to us; he sets himself against our doings. . . . Let us condemn him to a shameful death, for according to his own words, God will take care of him. . . . Their wickedness blinded them . . . ."

The Gospel spells out the gathering storm over Jesus. "He had decided not to travel in Judea because some of the Jews were looking for a chance to kill him." He goes anyway, but secretly. But before long he becomes visible. He stands up in the Temple and cries out: "So you know me, and you know my origins? The truth is, I have not come of myself. I was sent by One who has the right to send, and him you do not know." It sounds like blasphemy to them, so it is not hard to see why "they tried to seize him, but no one laid a finger on him because his hour had not yet come."

It would be a mistake to think of Jesus' Passion taking place only during the last three days of his last week. Those days were only the climax of a Passion that had been building up since the beginning of his public life. Every desertion of a follower, the misunderstanding of himself and his mission on the part of his chosen disciples, his being rejected by his own people at Nazareth—all contributed to the Passion of Jesus. Rejection, unbelief, scorn were no easier for him to accept than for us. But here at the end of his life he encounters hatred—most painful of all agonies, especially when one knows he doesn't deserve it. The psalmist's cry belongs to him in full right: "Save me, O God, by your power, and grant me justice! God, hear my prayer; listen to my plea" (Entrance Antiphon).

Jesus' human side, his emotions and feelings, were never more evident than during these last weeks of his life. And never did he pray more anxiously for deliverance and help, as will be evident at the Last Supper and in the Garden of Olives. The Responsorial

Psalm says that "the Lord is close to the brokenhearted; and those who are crushed in spirit he saves. Many are the troubles of the just man, but out of them all the Lord delivers him." The psalm was small comfort to him. Even on the cross he begged to know why the Father had abandoned him. When we suffer, it takes a lot of faith to believe that the Lord is close and that he will deliver us.

And yet, what alternative is there? So with Jesus we pray: "Father, our source of life, you know our weakness. May we reach out with joy to grasp your hand and walk more readily in your ways." It's a risky prayer—begging God that we might reach out *with joy* to grasp his hand and thus walk more readily in his ways, for we don't know where those ways will lead. But again, what is the alternative?

One thing we can thank Jesus for: the object lesson of how his own life ends. He sweats blood in the garden, he will be nailed to a cross, he will die on it, but after three days he will rise from the dead. "In Christ, through the shedding of his blood, we have redemption and forgiveness of our sins by the abundance of his grace" (Communion Antiphon). We'll have not only the forgiveness of sins but new life and understanding for this old one we are living now.

Today's meditation does not specifically emphasize the personal conversion we have been stressing up to now. But what could further that conversion more than the remembrance of all that Jesus has done for us and the goal he holds out to us? And so we pray: "Lord, in this eucharist we pass from death to life. Keep us from our old and sinful ways and help us to continue in the new life" (Prayer After Communion). We have to say *Amen* to that prayer. It sums up all of Lent.

* * *

"The wicked said among themselves: 'Let us beset the just one, because he is obnoxious to us; he sets himself against our doings'" (*Reading I*).

"The Lord is close to the brokenhearted; and those who are crushed in spirit he saves" (*Responsorial Psalm*).

READING I Jer 11:18-20
GOSPEL John 7:40-53

Reading I: Jeremiah's readiness to suffer related in this reading fits Jesus perfectly. He too will be a trusting lamb led to slaughter.

Gospel: The crowd is sharply divided over Jesus: Some think he is the Messiah, others that he is an imposter.

Today's liturgy takes us right into the heart of Jesus' Passion; the psalmist's words belong to him: "The snares of death overtook me, the ropes of hell tightened around me; in my distress I called upon the Lord, and he heard my voice" (Entrance Antiphon). We do not yet witness the physical torture Jesus endured, but the mental agony is well under way. The Father so loved the world that he sent his own Son, that all who believe in him might have eternal life (Gospel Verse); but what he is experiencing in today's Gospel doesn't seem much like a grateful welcome.

On the contrary, these little people, this crowd made up of his virulent enemies, of hangers-on, and a few who have the courage to tell how they feel about him and to defend him—this crowd for whom he will give his life sits in judgment over him. Jesus is tossed back and forth between those who hate him and those who want him to have a fair hearing. "No man ever spoke like that before," said the Temple guards—a defense of Jesus that is quickly destroyed by the judgment of the Pharisees: "You do not see any of the Sanhedrin believing in him, do you?" In a word, for them Jesus is a crook, a deceiver, a false prophet unworthy of anyone's trust. Does any human being enjoy being hated? Jesus, I repeat, is well advanced into his Passion. The snares of death are indeed overtaking him.

Jesus can make his own what had been foretold about him by the prophets both in their words and in their lives. Like Jeremiah he can say: "I knew their plot because the Lord informed me. . . . Yet I, like a trusting lamb led to slaughter, had not realized that they were hatching plots against me: 'Let us destroy the tree in its vigor; let us cut him off from the land of the living, so that his name will be spoken no more'" (Reading I). Knowing in advance what is plotted for him, makes him cry out the more: "Lord, my God, I take shelter in you. . . . Save me from my pursuers and rescue me. . . . Do me justice, O Lord, because I am just, and because of the innocence that is mine. Let the malice of the wicked come to an end" (Responsorial Psalm).

What about us? The Opening Prayer can give a hint: "Lord, guide us in your gentle mercy, for left to ourselves we cannot do your will." We do not generally do a very good job of doing God's will — not because he and his will have not been present to us — but mostly because we have not been present to him.

Today's readings and prayers again make us face up to our relationship with this Jesus in his Passion. It seems that we cannot escape seeing ourselves as members of the crowd confronting Jesus in today's Gospel. Whose side would we have been on? Undoubtedly, not on the side of the hate-filled Pharisees who have already condemned him. But what about all those indifferent ones who didn't care one way or another about Jesus and about what was happening to him? I repeat that the opposite of love is not hatred but indifference.

If indifference has been our problem, there is still time to take a stand. "*Make* our hearts obedient to your will," we pray in the Prayer over the Gifts. It's a prayer he will surely answer if we want it badly enough. And the statement of Peter in today's Communion Antiphon can surely help us there: "We have been ransomed with the precious blood of Christ, as with the blood of a lamb without blemish or spot." No one has ever spoken as he has, no one has ever lived as he did, no one has ever loved as he did, no one has ever deserved our love as he has.

* * *

"The snares of death overtook me, the ropes of hell tightened around me; in my distress I called upon the Lord, and he heard my voice" (*Entrance Antiphon*).

"God so loved the world that he gave us his only Son, that all who believe in him might have eternal life" (*Gospel Verse*).

READING I   Ezek 37:12-14   READING II   Rom 8:8-11
GOSPEL   John 11:1-45

Reading I: God promises to his people through Ezechiel that he will deliver them from oppression and restore them to freedom.

Reading II: If anyone does not have the Spirit of Christ, he does not belong to Christ, says St. Paul.

Gospel: John relates the event of the raising of Lazarus.

"Out of the depths I cry to you, O Lord; Lord, hear my voice! Let your ears be attentive to the voice of my supplication" (Responsorial Psalm). Such is the agonizing cry of suffering humankind through the ages. It was the cry of Jesus in his agony, of Martha and Mary at the loss of their brother Lazarus. And it is our cry now as we live, struggle, and agonize in our efforts to carry the cross of our own personal pain.

The anguish of loneliness, the pain of separation from loved ones, the threatened loss of someone dear to us, the worry and anxiety of those closest to our hearts, the concern about the future—in so many of us—all this pain is gathered up to force from our dread-filled hearts our personal *"De profundis . . . .* Out of the depths we cry to you, O Lord . . . ."

Jesus knows that pain better than we do. Pain like ours has wrenched countless healing miracles from his compassionate heart. And now, his being moved with deepest emotion, being troubled in spirit, his tears mingled with those of Martha, Mary, and their friends—all this was not an act. "See how much he loved him!" the people remarked when they saw him weep. The tears of Jesus now flow for us and for all who suffer everywhere. Lazarus is a symbol of agonizing humanity. And the same comment is as true today as it was there outside of Lazarus' tomb: "See how much he loved him!"

But Jesus did more than weep that day. He brought Lazarus back to life again, back face-to-face with Jesus. And just as Martha, Mary, and their friends are symbols of suffering humanity, so is Lazarus a symbol of humanity's deliverance, of our ultimate and final victory over sin, pain, suffering, and death. "I am the resurrection and the life, says the Lord: he who believes in me will not die for ever" (Gospel Verse). More immediately for us, Lazarus is a symbol of the goal of Lent—for the Church, for the catechumens, and for each of us who has been concerned not only with the pain of living but with our personal growing up and coming to new life at

Easter: our conversion, our becoming new again.

It is important for us to note who accomplishes all this: It is Jesus. The emphasis in all the readings and prayers is on him and his power and love and desire to heal. There is always a danger, especially in preaching and writing, of placing so much emphasis on human effort that we may too easily forget that the whole process of conversion is primarily God's grace in us, gratefully accepted by us. It is with the Lord that there is mercy and fullness of redemption (Responsorial Psalm), not with human striving and personal accomplishments. Jesus in the Gospel shows himself to us as love in person, and that manifestation requires a response from us. And that is where we come in. Responding to love from our hearts — responding with grateful personal love — that and that alone is our share in the process of all conversion . . . and remaining firmly fixed and even growing in that conversion.

Both of the opening prayers recognize our personal helplessness in the matter of coming to terms with suffering as well as with the lifelong process of conversion to which we are called, "Help us, Father, to be like Christ your Son, who loved the world and died for our salvation. Inspire us by his love and guide us by his example." And there is a very special plea in the Alternate Prayer: "Change our selfishness into self-giving. Help us to embrace the world you have given us, that we may transform the darkness of its pain into the life and joy of Easter."

What a dramatic change in the thinking of many Christians is demanded by that prayer! Too many religious people seem to despise the world and to want to absent themselves from it in order to live in an exclusively "spiritual" universe. There is a considerable difference between "secularism" or "worldliness" (which distracts us or blinds us to God as Creator of the world) and "embracing the world," as our prayer recommends . . . and which is not incompatible with the religious, even the contemplative, life, as the example of many saints shows us. Jesus himself in his life embraced the world and its people. To moralize a bit, maybe it is time for us to be ourselves, human beings, not angels — human beings aware of our dignity as human persons empowered by Christ to bring him more and more into human life on all levels: time for us to realize that when we absent ourselves from life, from loving appreciation of what God has given us in and through life, we actually separate ourselves from Jesus Christ. "See how he loved him!"

If eternity is life with God, if it is the full gratification of all the thirsts and hungers of our hearts for love, for life, for truth, it can and must begin now in this world. The Christian does not look on death as the pagan does — as the end of everything — or even as most bereaved people look on it. For the Christian death is the beginning of a new life, or more exactly, as the unfolding of a life that is already theirs once they are reborn in baptism and have Christ living in them.

The resurrection of Lazarus is a type of the resurrection of Jesus and also of our own twofold "resurrection" both at the renewal of our baptism at Easter and our final resurrection at the end of time. The raising of Lazarus, however, is not the same as that of Jesus, as we shall see later. Lazarus still possessed his own, old body. Jesus' resurrected body will be his, but also "transfigured," a "new creation." The raising of Lazarus points to, but does not fully describe, this deeper truth. Death gives way to life and ends in glory. So, too, our own lives, if we keep our eyes fixed on him who is our resurrection and our life.

Without actually realizing the full meaning of what he says as Jesus announces his return to Jerusalem, the Apostle Thomas becomes an excellent guide for entering into the spirit of the two weeks just ahead: "Let us go and die with him," he says. We all have within ourselves the seed of our final resurrection, but this seed has to be buried in the ground and die if it is to flower and bear fruit. This dying is not only at the end of our life in this world; it is now, during what remains of Lent.

And we are not alone. Paul assures us that we possess the Holy Spirit who guides us not only in the coming two weeks of our conversion process, but all our lives: "If the Spirit of him who raised Jesus from the dead dwells in you, then he who raised Christ from the dead will bring your mortal bodies to life also through the Spirit dwelling in you" (Reading II). May we all put our faith in that blessed Spirit!

* * *

"Change our selfishness into self-giving. Help us to embrace the world you have given us, that we may transform the darkness of its pain into the life and joy of Easter (*Opening Prayer*).

"Out of the depths I cry to you, O Lord, Lord, hear my voice" (*Responsorial Psalm*).

"I am the resurrection and the life, says the Lord; he who believes in me will not die forever" (*Gospel Verse*).

READING I   Jer 31:31-34   **READING II**   Heb 5:7-9
GOSPEL   John 12:20-33

Reading I: God tells the nature of the "new covenant" he will make with his people: "I will place my law within them, and write it upon their hearts."

Reading II: The reading gives the nature and effect of Jesus' sacrifice: Son though he was, he learned obedience from what he suffered.

Gospel: Jesus shows us the law of life: The grain of wheat must fall to the earth and die if it is to bring forth fruit. He speaks of himself.

I am convinced that the greatest cause of unhappiness in the world is not pain or sorrow or loss of loved ones, but an unforgiving heart, a heart consumed with hatred and anger. Such a heart is wounded terribly, and unless its possessor *desires* and *seeks* healing from Jesus, its final fate can be frightening.

Whether our hearts are unforgiving or just plain weighed down with worry and pain of whatever kind, we need today's Mass, we need the Jesus whom today's liturgy presents to us. He is presented to us today as healer, supreme among all healers, but the answer he gives for the needs of our hearts may not seem at first to be what we are looking for.

The Gospel situates us at the beginning of Jesus' last week before his death. Among the crowds gathering for the Passover are some Greeks who tell Philip: "Sir, we should like to see Jesus." Who wouldn't like to see Jesus? Philip eventually gets the message to Jesus, whose answer was hardly what the poor Greeks expected:

The hour has come
for the Son of Man to be glorified.
I solemnly assure you,
unless the grain of wheat falls to the earth and dies,
it remains just a grain of wheat.
But if it dies,
it produces much fruit.
The man who loves his life
loses it,
while the man who hates his life in this world
preserves it to life eternal.

I believe what Jesus is saying is this: "If you really want to see me, if you want to see the real Jesus, Jesus as he *is*, the only way to do it is to see him as a divine seed that goes into the ground and dies;

but in the very process of dying, he shall arise a new being, a new seed, and will bring forth new and abundant other seeds." But we have to be careful here. Jesus is not like a seed that dies in order to bring forth new grain. He *is* the seed. The seed is a person, and what Jesus is telling us here is more than a moral lesson that warns us that we have to be humble and must mortify ourselves so that we can bear fruits of holiness.

What he is telling us is that if we want to see Jesus as he actually is, dying to self is the only way to do it. And that's what we will be doing in the next two weeks. In these weeks we are not mere bystanders or spectators at a long-past event. On the contrary, we are to enter into Christ's Passion and death now in and through our lives and our sufferings. The seed is Christ—the whole Christ, himself and us, his members. The whole Christ has to go into the ground and die, but if this seed dies, and only if it dies, it will yield a rich harvest. "If you serve me, follow me," says Jesus, "where I am there will my servant be." He is speaking about us, to us. Christ's Passion and death are ours, and our passion and suffering and dying are his. We are never alone, for he is with us and we with him.

The words of Jesus about the seed dying are applicable not only to following the liturgy in the next two weeks but also, and more particularly, to the penitential experience that we will want to enter into soon, namely, our Easter confession. In all the sacraments we die in order to live the risen life of Jesus with him and with one another, but this is especially the case with the sacrament of reconciliation.

Lent, particularly these last two weeks, is a good time for us to refresh our minds and hearts on this sacrament, especially in the context of the conversion experience we are engaged in. For this, it is important that we reflect on the so-called firm purpose of amendment that remains so essential an element in this sacrament. It is the element that we have the most trouble carrying out. How often have we gone to confession in years past? We used to go every month, maybe every week, but nothing seemed to happen in our lives. What was wrong? Why was our firm purpose of amendment so ineffectual? Was it simply that our human nature was so weak? Were we possibly making more progress than we thought? Was simply *wanting* to be better persons enough to satisfy the requirements of the sacrament? There was probably some truth in each of these "explanations."

Now I am beginning to wonder if we did not rely too much on our feeble human efforts and not enough on the saving power of Jesus inherent in the sacrament. We didn't see confession as a personal *entering into* the Passion, death, and resurrection of Jesus, as a miniature Lent and Holy week condensed and contracted into a few moments of confrontation with the healing Christ in the sacrament.

The reformed rite for the sacrament of reconciliation not only provides us with a new and wonderfully descriptive name for the sacrament, but it also provides both the confessor and the penitent with the opportunity to discern the promptings of the Holy Spirit in the penitent's life situation. This is not as forbidding as it sounds. It may simply mean an effort to agree on a program of a deeper prayer life which will rely to a great extent on the nourishment of the word of God. It may also mean a greater effort to lay bare the causes and reasons for our faults. Above all, it involves the awakening of a stronger desire to respond to the Jesus who presents himself to us daily as the most deserving in all the world of our love and desire.

So, in confession we are still to be concerned about seeking forgiveness for past sins, but now the orientation is also, perhaps most predominantly, to the future, to the new life of growth with and in the Risen Lord. And seen in the light of the immense love of Jesus manifested in his Passion and death for us, our firm purpose of amendment is now more than anything else our own love-response to him, a response which we demonstrate more and more in a life of greater mutual love for one another, in compassion for other sinners, in a deeper spirit of forgiveness and desire for reconciliation with those we have offended or who have offended us.

But what is the ultimate goal of everything—of these next two weeks, of Easter, of our daily Mass, our future confessions, and our life together? It is the ideal that the Lord presents to us in the First Reading today—that new covenant with us, God's people now, which is still and always in the process of being perfected; this new covenant in which he will place his law of love within us and write it on our hearts; the new covenant in which God will once and for all be our God and we shall at long last truly be his people. "No longer will they have need to teach their friends and kinsmen how to know the Lord. All, from least to greatest, shall know me, says the Lord, for I will forgive their evildoing and remember their sin no more."

"Create a clean heart in me, O God, and a steadfast spirit renew within me. Cast me not out of your presence, and your holy spirit take not from me, Amen."

* * *

"I will place my law within them and write it upon their hearts; I will be their God and they shall be my people" *(Reading I)*.

"A clean heart create for me, O God, and a steadfast spirit renew within me" *(Responsorial Psalm).*

"If anyone would serve me, let him follow me; where I am, there will my servant be" *(Gospel).*

FIFTH SUNDAY OF LENT   Cycle C

READING I   Isa 43:16-21   READING II   Phil 3:8-14
GOSPEL   John 8:1-11

Reading I: God asks his people not to long for the past but to open themselves to the future and the great promise of a better life he is
planning for them.

Reading II: "I have been grasped by Christ," says St. Paul. Therefore he
looks ahead to living with Christ and for him.

Gospel: Jesus forgives the woman taken in adultery and tells her to try
to reform her life.

"Remember not the events of the past, the things of long ago consider not; see, I am doing something new" (Reading I).

If there is one word that characterizes Lent, and especially what
remains of it, it is *newness*, new life, a new way of life. To give us
this newness, to recreate us — this is what God must be allowed to do
for us in whatever remains of this holy season. Today's readings and
prayers call us to this newness. We are called to leave the past
behind and to start a new life. It is not just a summons to individuals
but to the entire people of God. God speaks to *us* through the
prophet Isaiah: "For I put water in the desert and rivers in the
wasteland for my chosen people to drink, the people whom I formed
for myself, that they might announce my praise" (Reading I).

If we want some idea of what this newness should consist in, all
we have to do is meditate on the Second Reading from Paul: "I have
come to rate all as loss in the light of the surpassing knowledge of my
Lord Jesus Christ. For his sake I have forfeited everything; I have
accounted all else rubbish so that Christ may be my wealth and I
may be in him . . . . I wish to know Christ and the power flowing
from his resurrection; likewise to know how to share in his sufferings

by being formed into the pattern of his death. Thus do I hope that I may arrive at resurrection from the dead."

So our conversion, its goal, the new life we can look forward to, is much more than a quest for morality or ethics in our lives: not just doing good, but above all *being* good, that is, being in Christ and knowing him as he is, making his mind our own. And this is not primarily our achievement: It is Christ himself working the miracle of change within us . . . if we are willing to turn ourselves over to him and are willing to cooperate with him in rooting out the obstacles within that work against his dominating our minds and hearts.

As usual, the Gospel is the center of this moment of our Lenten pilgrimage. There are two ways of looking at the Gospel (as with most of the Gospels of the year): first, in its original historical setting in the day-by-day unfolding of the life of Jesus in Palestine. Then, and more importantly, looking at it and its meaning—the reason why it is being used at this particular moment in the year, in Lent. Today's Gospel about the woman taken in adultery and dragged before Jesus contains minor and major features. For us to concentrate on how often we resemble the Pharisees in judging others can make us feel guilty for a moment, but it would be to miss the whole point of the choice of this Gospel for *this* Lenten Sunday.

The focus is on the sinful woman and what Jesus does for her. She is the one the Church wants us to identify with today and always. What feelings of terror, anger, fear, guilt, and lostness she must experience as she cringes in the midst of the hate-filled crowd! But there is one there who does not hate, who does not condemn— one who pities instead, who understands human weakness and forgives. Everyone else condemns her, despises her, and she probably condemns and despises herself. But Jesus, instead of condemning, becomes her defender and wins her acquittal. "Woman," he says to her when all her judges have slunk away, "where did they all disappear to? Has no one condemned you?" "No one, Sir," she answers. Jesus said, "Nor do I condemn you. You may go. But from now on, avoid this sin."

I think she will obey Jesus and avoid the sin, but she will never leave him, nor he her. They will henceforth be present one to the other. What Jesus did for her was to restore her dignity, her self-esteem. No one had ever believed in her before, so she could not believe in herself. But Jesus believed in her. That's always the way it is with him and the Father. God's love and merciful forgiveness never degrades us as persons. On the contrary it lifts us up and assures us that we are supremely loved, even when we think we are unlovable. The more misery and sin abound, the more do divine mercy and forgiveness abound.

"See, I am doing something new!" says the Lord, and the nameless adulteress knows what he is talking about. And she can make her own the words of the Responsorial Psalm: "The Lord has done great things for me, I am filled with joy." Now a new life is open to her and possible for her. Her life can never be what it used to be. This is conversion in its best and most beautiful sense.

The experience of this nameless woman must be our experience now and especially during what remains of Lent. We have probably not been guilty of such a sin as hers, and, above all, we have not been caught at it. No matter. Sin is sin, and undoubtedly we all have a backlog to reflect upon. But we should not reflect too much, certainly not to reflect so much that we lose sight of the forgiving Jesus who stands over us, believes in us, loves us, and forgives us again and again. "Remember not the events of the past, the things of long ago consider not; see, I am doing something new!" That new something God is doing in us is all that matters.

But we can return to the woman for the last time. We can even wonder about her life after this dramatic confrontation with Jesus, wonder whether or not she ever fell again. After all, she was human and capable of being tempted, capable also of falling. But for the time being, we can be sure that between her and Jesus there exists a relationship she never knew or experienced before. I don't suppose she could put it in words, but St. Paul, reflecting on his own conversion, on what Jesus did for him, does it for her (and for us): "I have come to rate all as loss in the light of the surpassing knowledge of my Lord Jesus Christ." "The Lord has done great things for us; we are filled with joy."

* * *

"Father, help us to be like Christ who loved the world and died for our salvation. Inspire us by his love, guide us by his example" (Opening Prayer).

"Remember not the things of the past, the things of long ago consider not; see, I am doing something new" (Reading I).

"I do not wish the sinner to die, says the Lord, but to turn to me and live" (Gospel Verse).

READING I   Dan 13:1-9, 15-17, 19-30, 33-62
GOSPEL   John 8:1-11

Reading I: We hear the story of Susanna falsely accused of adultery and rescued by the boy named Daniel.

Gospel: Jesus forgives the sin of a woman taken in adultery and rescues her from certain death at the hands of her accusers.

The two readings for today correspond almost perfectly. Two women are accused of adultery and are about to be stoned to death. But at the last moment they are rescued by "saviors," Daniel in the one case, Jesus in the other. Susanna is innocent and unjustly accused. The terrified woman standing before Jesus is guilty and justly accused, at least according to the Law (she was caught in the act; we can wonder what happened to the man!).

"God, have pity on me! My enemies are crushing me; all day long they wage war on me" (Entrance Antiphon). This plea belongs to the women in the readings, it belongs to Jesus, also innocently accused and about to be condemned to death; it can belong to us as well, even if our enemy is only our own tendency to sin or our daily cross.

There may be some Christians who wonder what in the world these readings are doing in our Lenten Masses. As a matter of fact, both readings have embarrassed some delicate-hearted people through the ages, and some have even wanted to see them deleted from Scripture . . . a fact that indicates how little they know about God and the teaching of Jesus, his Son. It is no coincidence that the psalm chosen for our response to the reading about Susanna is Psalm 23: "The Lord is my shepherd; I shall not want. . . . Even though I walk in the dark valley I fear no evil; for you are at my side."

The truth is that both these readings are part of our Christian heritage: They are *good news*, for they tell of God's unconditional, unmerited forgiving love, not only for the good and innocent but for all sinners, great or small. "I do not wish the sinner to die, says the Lord, but to turn to me and live" (Gospel Verse).

What has all this to do with us? Depending on our background, we can identify with either of these two women. And so much the better if we can identify with either of the rescuers, Jesus or Daniel. The truth is that we ourselves were rescued from death by Jesus when he saw to it that we were baptized. But there have been relapses, so we have been trying to come back to him during this Lenten season. We still need—indeed, we always will need—

constant help in order to remain "rescued." And that makes all of to-day's prayers particularly appropriate: "Father of love, source of all blessing, help us to pass from our old life of sin to the new life of grace" (Opening Prayer); "Lord, as we come with joy to celebrate the mystery of the eucharist, may we offer you hearts purified by bodily penance" (Prayer over the Gifts); "Father, through the grace of your sacraments, *may we follow Christ more faithfully* and come to the joy of your kingdom" (Prayer After Communion).

So Lent sums up and characterizes all of life. There is defeat, sin, rescue, relapse, progress and growth, more relapse, final victory. So will it always be. But the essential thing is that we have Jesus for our rescuer, Jesus who says to us again and again: "Has no one con-demned you? . . . Nor do I condemn you. You may go, but from now on, avoid this sin."

And we will go, but since we are so weak and there is so much pressure on us from the world around us, we shall probably fall again. But he will always be there, always forgiving, never con-demning, telling us over and over that he does not will our death but that we turn to him and live. He spreads his table before us in the sight of our foes, anoints us with oil and fills our cup of gladness to overflowing. And finally, one day his love and grace will win through and we will follow him more faithfully and come to the joy of his kingdom. And we will dwell in the house of the Lord in years to come.

* * *

"Though I walk in the valley of darkness, I fear no evil, for you are with me" *(Responsorial Psalm)*.

"Let the man among you who has no sin be the first to cast a stone at her" *(Gospel)*.

"Has no one condemned you? The woman answered: No one, Lord. Neither do I condemn you: go and do not sin again" *(Communion Antiphon)*.

READING I   Num 21:4-9
GOSPEL   John 8:21-30

Reading I: Punished by the bites of serpents for grumbling against Moses, the Israelites are saved by gazing upon a serpent raised on a pole.

Gospel: We hear the continuation of the confrontation between Jesus and his enemies. Jesus predicts his being lifted up, but he knows that the Father has not deserted him because he always does the Father's will.

Again there is near-perfect correspondence between the two readings. The Israelites grumble against Moses and are punished by biting serpents, but they are delivered by gazing upon a bronze serpent erected by Moses, following the directives of the Lord. Humankind has sinned, become estranged from God, but is rescued by Jesus lifted up on the cross. "The Lord looked down from his holy height . . . to release those doomed to die" (Responsorial Psalm).

Jesus foretells this rescue in one of his final discussions with his enemies: "When you lift up the Son of Man, you will come to realize that I AM and that I do nothing by myself. . . . The One who sent me is with me. He has not deserted me since *I always do what pleases him.*" I have stressed those last words, because they again repeat the entire dynamic motivation of Jesus' redeeming life and death, namely, total obedience to the will of the Father. "I AM," claims Jesus. He uses the very words that God himself used when he identified himself to Moses at the burning bush. To his enemies this makes him guilty of blasphemy. But on the other hand, John says, "Because he spoke this way, many came to believe in him."

Later in John's Gospel (ch 12), Jesus will enlarge on the prophecy he makes today: "When I am lifted up from the earth, I will draw all men to myself" (Communion Antiphon). That includes *all of us.* It's a fascinating statement. We may wonder if every person born into the world has actually experienced the pull of Jesus, lifted up on the cross. That may be idle curiosity. But what is not idle is to examine whether or not we feel personally drawn ourselves, how strong the pull is, and whether or not we have given in to it.

We probably hold back a little, for instinctively we realize that by giving in to the magnet of the crucified Christ, we may end up on the cross ourselves. Giving in to the attraction of Jesus means making our own his words: "I do always what pleases him." In a word, the will of the Father — with all its potential for suffering — becomes the personal desire of our minds, our hearts, our whole being. It means faith in the sense of total consent, trust, abandon, full willingness to allow God to love us as he loved his own Son.

The Church recognizes this essential element in the meaning of Christianity in today's Opening Prayer: "Lord, help us to do your will that your Church may grow and become more faithful to your service." This prayer makes a fascinating deduction: The growth of the Church depends on our fidelity to the will of the Father. But why not, since fidelity to the will of the Father is precisely what animated Jesus and brought the Church into existence in the first place?

But back to that cross with its divine victim and his power to pull us to himself. It might well be that the Greek writer Nikos Kazantzakis has found the best application of Jesus' words in his description of "three kinds of souls, three kinds of prayers":

> I am a bow in your hands, Lord, draw me lest I rot.
> Do not overdraw me, Lord, I shall break.
> Overdraw me, Lord, and who cares if I break?
>
> (*Report to Greco*, New York: Bantam Books, 1965, 11)

These three prayers pretty well characterize most of us who claim to be followers of Christ. We do want to belong to Christ, but too often our courage falters. We fear being asked to do or endure too much pain. But we keep on desiring. We don't give up because God does not give up on us. One of these years, one of these Lents, we will at long last allow ourselves to be captured by his love and then we will make the final leap and cry out: "Overdraw me, Lord, and who cares if I break?"

* * *

"Put your hope in the Lord. Take courage and be strong" (*Entrance Antiphon*).

"Hide not your face from me in the day of my distress. Incline your ear to me; in the day when I call, answer me speedily" (*Responsorial Psalm*).

"When I am lifted up from the earth, I will draw all men to myself, says the Lord" (*Communion Antiphon*).

READING I   Dan 3:14-20, 91-92, 95
GOSPEL   John 8:31-42

Reading I: Three Hebrew youths who refuse to worship an idol are condemned to death but rescued by God. Their steadfastness wins the grace of faith for the king.

Gospel: The argument between Jesus and his enemies continues. Jesus turns their own claims against them.

The story of the three young men in the fiery furnace is so familiar to us from song and legend that we too easily pass over its deep meaning. The king threatens the three with death if they refuse to worship the golden statue he has set up. Their response to the threat is simple and noble: "If our God, whom we serve, can save us from the white-hot furnace and from your hands, O king, may he save us! But even if he will not, know, O king, that we will not serve your god or worship the golden statue." Their God means more to them than their lives.

God rewards their fidelity. He rescues them and more than that he shows them that their loyalty to the one true God becomes the occasion for the conversion of the king himself, who cries out: "Blessed be the God of Shadrach, Meshack and Abednego, who sent his angel to deliver his servants that trust in him." Both for the catechumens and for us, the loyalty of the three young men is a magnificent example of how to make fidelity to conscience an act of worship and of grace for those in need.

The Gospel continues the confrontation between Jesus and his enemies. The issue is again human freedom. "If you live according to my teaching, you are truly my disciples; then you will know the truth. and the truth will set you free." That principle is as much for us as for Christ's antagonists, who choose not to understand him. Even if truth is liberating, they choose not to understand Jesus. He goes on to tell them that membership in the Chosen People does not make them God's friends; it is not the heart of religion. To know that heart, they have to look to Abraham, whom they claim as their father, whose entire life was an act of faith, of trust; and they have to make that faith their own.

Their claim to be children of Abraham and then of God himself cannot hold up in the face of their refusal to follow Abraham's example of true faith. They reject Jesus' claim to have come forth from God. Their unbelieving attitude contrasts drastically with that of the three youths who are so eager to stand up for the supremacy of

God. They come off badly even if contrasted with King Nebuchadnezzar, who gave in to God's grace and became a gracious fellow-believer with his would-be victims.

Once again we have to enter personally into this liturgy and find meaning in it for ourselves. St. Paul is a good guide: "God has transformed us into the kingdom of the Son he loves; in him we are redeemed, and find forgiveness" (Communion Antiphon). That's the bare fact of our baptism and its initial effect. But there is another fact that has to be taken into account: It is that of our human freedom, with all its potential either for attaching us to our God in love and fidelity or for trying to use God for our own advantage.

The prayers of this Mass not only reveal us to ourselves, but also they give words to the problems that enter our lives as a result of the misuse of our freedom. "Father of mercy, hear the prayers of your repentant children who call on you in love. Enlighten our minds and sanctify our hearts" (Opening Prayer). Enlightenment of minds and sanctification of hearts might well be the most basic need of our lives. Once again our Lenten life is summed up. The enlightenment we need, of course, is that which the three youths possessed: a clear vision of the Lord's complete supremacy over their lives, together with the acknowledgement of that supremacy in praiseful worship.

Sin is sin whether it be that of Nabuchadnezzar or of the enemies of Jesus or our own. The only remedy is a sanctified heart, and the only one who can bring that off is God himself and by means of the Eucharist and the other sacraments Jesus has given us. And so we end with the best prayer of all: "Lord, may the mysteries we receive heal us, remove sin from our hearts, and make us strong under your constant protection."

* * *

"Lord, you rescue me from raging enemies, you lift me up above my attackers, you deliver me from violent men" *(Entrance Antiphon)*.

"Happy are they who have kept the word with a generous heart, and yield a harvest through perseverance" *(Gospel Verse)*.

"God has transferred us into the kingdom of the Son he loves; in him we are redeemed, and find forgiveness of our sins" *(Communion Antiphon)*.

READING I   Gen 17:3-9
GOSPEL   John 8:51-59

Reading I: God changes Abram's name to Abraham, establishes a covenant with him, and promises to make him the "father of a host of nations."

Gospel: "Before Abraham came to be, I AM," Jesus declares, and his enemies make ready to stone him for blasphemy.

If one failed to remember that with God there is no past and no future but only the eternal present, one might be tempted to conjecture that today's readings must bring back a lot of memories for him. Memories or not, God's heart must still take delight in this good man Abraham, whom he chose to be the father of his people and with whom he made that first covenant. Abraham never let the Lord down.

The theme of covenant runs through all of today's Mass, and surely it is the most basic idea about Christianity for the catechumens (and for us born Christians) to concentrate on and always to remember. Covenant means *alliance*, a joining together of parties that is permanent. The analogy God himself used in the Old Testament was the contract of marriage between a man and a woman. The essence of the covenant is love. Without love a marriage can hardly last, and neither can the covenant between God and his people. The very language of Reading I suggests a marriage contract with its mutual obligations.

God changed Abram's name as a sign of his new vocation as a partner in the covenant. God will be the God of Abram and his descendants, he will protect them, give them a new fatherland. All they have to do is to acknowledge God as Lord of all, Lord of their lives. "Look to the Lord in his strength; seek to serve him constantly" (Responsorial Psalm).

One of the best ways of keeping a marriage fresh and lasting is by celebrating anniversaries year after year. The celebration makes the husband and wife *remember* their first love. God knows the human heart; he knows its need to remember. Without remembering, love grows cold and may even vanish. He himself never forgets: "The Lord remembers his covenant for ever." And so he tells his people: "Recall the wondrous deeds the Lord has wrought."

In our baptism we too received a new name which indicates our new vocation as members of a covenant people, the Church. It is as members of this covenant people that we approach God in prayer, in worship, in the fidelity of daily life. Our life as members of the covenant people has to be a life of faith, like that of our father Abraham, a life of care and love for our fellow members of the covenant, like that of our Savior Jesus who died for love of us all, a life of total obedience to the loving will of God our Father.

The covenant God initially made with Abraham, he reinforced with Moses, and it reaches its ultimate realization in Jesus. "Christ is the mediator of a new covenant so that, since he has died, those who are called may receive the eternal inheritance promised to them" (Entrance Antiphon). A week from today is Holy Thursday, the day of the Lord's Supper, that Passover meal at which Jesus instituted the Eucharist, which St. Paul describes thus:

> I have received from the Lord what I also delivered to you, that the Lord Jesus on the night when he was betrayed took bread, and when he had given thanks, he broke it, and said, "This is my body which is for you. DO THIS IN REMEMBRANCE OF ME." In the same way also the cup, after supper, saying, "This cup is THE NEW COVENANT in my blood. DO THIS, AS OFTEN AS YOU DRINK IT, IN REMEMBRANCE OF ME." For as often as you eat this bread and drink the cup, you proclaim the Lord's death until he comes (1 Cor 11:23-26).

"The Lord remembers his covenant forever." He wants us to remember, too, for unless we do, we lose our identity as a covenant people. The Eucharist is essentially a *covenant meal* that makes present his entire life, death, and resurrection. The Eucharist helps us to keep in mind that our greatest treasure is Jesus, whom God gave to us as the mediator of our new covenant: "God did not spare his own Son, but gave him up for us all; with Christ he will surely give us all things" (Communion Antiphon). To which we can only respond: "THANKS BE TO GOD!"

* * *

"Christ is the mediator of the new covenant so that, since he died, those who are called may receive the eternal inheritance promised to them" (Entrance Antiphon).

"The Lord remembers his covenant forever" (Responsorial Psalm).

READING I   Jer 20:10-13
GOSPEL   John 10:31-42

Reading I: Jeremiah's fearful reflections on the antagonism of his enemies could well be that of Jesus himself at the prospect of his own death.

Gospel: Jesus' enemies accuse him of blasphemy for claiming to be God. But his "hour" has not yet arrived, and he escapes their violence.

Today's Entrance Antiphon rises up from the heart of anguished humanity, including each of us; most of all it comes from the heart of humanity's head, Jesus the Lord: "Have mercy on me, Lord, for I am in distress; rescue me from the hands of my enemies. Lord keep me from shame, for I have called on you."

Both readings depict a hero beset by enemies who are filled with hatred and murderous intent. The Responsorial Psalm gives words to the distress within both Jesus and Jeremiah: "The breakers of death surged round about me, the destroying floods overwhelmed me . . . . In my distress I called upon the Lord, and cried out to my God; from his temple he heard my voice, and my cry to him reached his ears." We know, however, that one week from today, on Good Friday, Christ's enemies will prevail; they will kill him. But their "victory" will only be temporary. He will rise again. "Sing to the Lord, praise the Lord, for he has rescued the life of the poor from the power of the wicked" (Reading I).

But we can leave history and enter into the present: God wants us to consider these texts in terms of our own lives now. The historical texts tell us what happened to Jeremiah and Jesus then. Now they provide the background for what is going on in our midst now: in the Church, in our world, in our own lives. Who can estimate the vast amount of suffering in the world today—the agony of innocent children, the ravages of natural catastrophes, the anxiety of parents at the loss of beloved children?

We ourselves are attacked and besieged today even as Jesus and Jeremiah were then. We are both victims and our own worst enemies. By our deliberate sins we diminish ourselves as persons, and we continue to add to the tide of evil in the world which would certainly destroy us were it not for Christ's original victory on that first Easter. Our sins of commission and omission—our hatreds, our refusal to forgive, our coldness towards others, our unconcern for others' needs: All are crimes against the living Christ. With good reason we pray in the Opening Prayer: "Lord, grant us your forgiveness, and set us free from our enslavement to sin."

Free us, too, and perhaps most of all, from our indifference to suffering around us and everywhere in our world. The Communion Antiphon tells us that "Jesus carried our sins in his own body on the cross so that we could die to sin and live in holiness; by his wounds we have been healed." Yes, we have indeed been healed in the sense that humanity is again reconciled to the Father. But we are not personally healed unless and until we accept the healing, allow it to penetrate to the innermost corners of our hearts, do all in our power to remain healed . . . and then do all in our power to share Christ's healing with others. There is a bumper sticker on some cars which says: "Have Christ — Will Share." May it be true, may it be true of all of us!

* * *

"Have mercy on me, Lord, for I am in distress; rescue me from the hands of my enemies. Lord, keep me from shame, for I have called to you" (Entrance Antiphon).

"In my distress I called upon the Lord, and he heard my voice" (Responsorial Psalm).

257   SATURDAY OF THE FIFTH WEEK OF LENT

READING I   Ezek 37:21-28
GOSPEL   John 11:45-57

Reading I: Ezechiel foretells God's restoring the people to their land and his promise to dwell with them and be their God.

Gospel: Without realizing what he says, Caiaphas decrees that it is expedient that one man should die for his people.

The Vigil of Easter, the night during which the catechumens are to be baptized, the moment they have so longed for, is only a week away — a fact that is reflected in our readings today. "God our Father, you always work to save us, and now we rejoice in the great love you give to your chosen people. Protect all who are about to become your children, and continue to bless those who are already baptized" (Opening Prayer). The prayer expresses our desires as well as those of the prospective new Christians. The fact of our having already been chosen to become members of God's people, the Church, has always been considered a sign of the deep, personal love that he has for us. "The Lord will guard us, like a shepherd guarding his flock" (Responsorial Psalm).

But today's readings, especially the Gospel, have other wonderful nourishment for our hearts. The Gospel plants us right in the midst of the deadly intrigue that is surely going to destroy Jesus. Jesus has just raised Lazarus from the dead, causing many Jews to put their faith in him. The Sanhedrin becomes frantic. "What are we going to do," they said, "with this man performing all sorts of signs?"

Caiaphas, the high priest of that year, has no doubts about what needs to be done: "You have no understanding whatever!" he tells his confreres in the Sanhedrin. "Can you not see that it is better for you to have one man die (for the people) than to have the whole nation destroyed?" To which the evangelist adds the significant commentary: "He did not say this on his own. It was rather as high priest for that year that he prophesied that Jesus would die for the nation—and not for this nation only, but to gather into one all the dispersed children of God."

The scattering of peoples and the resulting antagonism between them was one of the deadliest consequences of the original fall of humankind, of its rebellion against the Lord. To restore the original unity among peoples and between them and their God is certainly one of the chief works of the Messiah, and if we look around us, we see that there is still an awful lot to be done.

The prophet Ezechiel adds to the evangelist's comment and in doing so takes us into those mysterious messianic times at the world's end, when the work begun by Jesus will reach ultimate fulfillment. God says through the prophet: "My dwelling will be with them; I will be their God, and they shall be my people. Thus the nations shall know that it is I, the Lord, who make Israel holy, when my sanctuary shall be set up among them forever." And the psalmist adds: "He who scattered Israel, now gathers them together; he guards them as a shepherd his flock. . . . Then the virgins shall make merry and dance, and young men and old as well. I will turn their mourning into joy, I will console and gladden them after their sorrows" (Responsorial Psalm).

It is obvious that unity among all peoples is the ideal for which

Jesus died and rose again. We recall his own words, "When I am lifted up from the earth, I will draw all men to myself" (John 12:32). In him we will all be one! Praise God! It is an ideal that he makes possible by his death and resurrection.

But he places the carrying out of that ideal into our hands, makes it our responsibility. Human beings cause division. Theirs is the task of working with him to restore it. That task causes us all to reflect on our need of the words of the Gospel salutation: "Rid yourselves of all your sins; and make a new heart and a new spirit."

* * *

"The Lord will guard us, like a shepherd guarding his flock" (*Responsorial Psalm*).

"Christ was sacrificed so that he could gather together the scattered children of God" (*Communion Antiphon*).

37   PASSION SUNDAY (Palm Sunday)

READING I   Isa 50:4-7   READING II   Phil 2:6-11
GOSPEL   Matt 26:14-27; 27:11-54

Reading I: We hear Isaiah's prophecy of the Servant of the Lord's willingness to give himself over to the suffering his enemies plan for him.

Reading II: St. Paul summarizes Christ's life: He was God but humbled himself and became man, obediently accepting death and in the end being exalted.

Gospel: We hear the detailed description of the Passion of Jesus as seen by Matthew.

Today's readings and prayers compress all of Holy Week into a single celebration. It begins in triumph with the enthusiastic entrance of Jesus into the Holy City, Jerusalem. In between there is tragedy and defeat, ending in death for Sunday's Hero. But it ends again in greater triumph than could ever have been imagined. And we share in it all. We have to be convinced that we are *not play-*

acting. We are celebrating and participating in a present reality— the death and resurrection of Jesus, our King and our Lord, made present here for us to share in and give our consent to.

We begin with the blessing of palms or branches from trees: "Lord, increase the faith of your people . . . . Today we honor Christ our triumphant King by carrying these branches. May we honor you every day by living always in him." The Gospel is read, and it is not difficult to envision the triumphant parade into the city, with Jesus riding on a donkey, the huge crowd spreading their cloaks on the ground, and the children waving their branches and reeds, crying: "Hosannah! Blessed is he who comes in the name of the Lord!"

Parades and processions have always been part of worship in Jewish and Christian tradition. They are the most normal way for the people to acclaim the victories and triumphs of their heroes and heroines. The people greet the hero with shouts and songs accompanied by instruments, and in so doing they seem to be able to take a vicarious pleasure and satisfaction in the hero's triumphant achievement. They share in it, almost as though they themselves had done what he had done. The accomplishment of the hero is in a strange way made present to the crowd.

When a parade is over in American cities, the heroes or heroines usually fade away and are forgotten. But not Jesus Christ whom we acclaim in today's parade. He will fade momentarily into his Passion and death, but then he will rise again from the dead and live on. He lives today in our midst. Year after year, he again leads us into the Holy City, up to the mount of Calvary, to die with him and rise again with him. Today Jesus lives, he lives now more than ever, and we follow and live with him. Remember that prayer for the blessing of palms: "May we honor you [Father] every day by living always in him [Jesus]. . . ."

Jesus also speaks to us in today's Mass, and his communication is very special. Using the expression of the Suffering Servant of Second Isaiah, he says to us: "The Lord has given me a well-trained tongue, that I might know how to speak to the weary a word that will rouse them. . . . I gave my back to those who beat me . . . my face I did not shield from buffets and spitting" (Reading I). During this Mass and all during Holy Week Jesus will speak to our human condition, our life, with all that it contains of mystery, sorrow, anguish, anxiety, worry, work (or lack of it).

But in speaking and showing himself to us in all his agony, he wants more than a momentary stirring of our emotions of pity and sorrow. He wants understanding and above all sharing. And he uses

St. Paul to tell us how to achieve this understanding and sharing: "Your attitude must be that of Christ (The old translation had it: "Have *this mind* in you which was also in Christ Jesus"). Though he was God, he did not deem equality with God a thing to be grasped at. Rather, "He emptied himself, and took the form of a slave. . . ."

He was willing to give up everything, even life itself, in total trust in the Father. It is that mind, that mentality, that we must seek to penetrate and to make our own. Doing that—seeking to understand and to accept as our own Christ's own thinking—is the one thing that will give meaning and purpose to our lives and help us to become "coredeemers" with Christ our head. This implies emptying ourselves of our own will, our desire to control our lives. It is faith, trust, total obedience to the will of the Father. We all know that being sincere in this desire is not easy. But God will give it if we want it badly enough.

So . . . may we all be open to Jesus, to his thinking, his desire; open to the word he speaks to us today and throughout this week. Above all, may we have our hearts open to the love for the Father and for us that will inspire all that we do this week and in the years to come. For it is only on condition that we share in his mind, his obedience, that we will be sure to experience the triumph of Jesus at Easter and make that triumph our own.

> Father, you have given the human race Jesus Christ our Savior as a model of humility. He fulfilled your will by becoming man and giving his life on the cross. Help us to bear witness to you by following his example of suffering and make us worthy to share in his resurrection (Prayer of the Mass).

* * *

"Hosanna to the Son of David, the King of Israel. Blessed is he who comes in the name of the Lord. Hosanna in the highest" (*Opening Antiphon*).

"Christ became obedient for us even to death, dying on the cross. Therefore God raised him on high and gave him a name above all other names" (*Gospel Verse*).

"Father, if this cup may not pass, but I must drink it, then your will be done" (*Communion Antiphon*).

READING I   **Isa 42:1-7**
GOSPEL   **John 12:1-11**

Reading I: We hear at first of the Servant Songs from Isaiah — a prophecy of the Servant's suffering, which will result in salvation for all.

Gospel: John relates the details of Jesus' last visit in the home of Martha, Mary, and Lazarus: Martha cooks, Mary pours out her precious ointment, Lazarus watches.

We may wonder if this first of the Servant Songs from Isaiah (Reading I) is not one of the Father's favorite Scripture passages: "Here is my servant whom I uphold, my chosen one with whom I am pleased." He uses practically the same words when Jesus is baptized in the River Jordan. Today's reading tells what the Father expects Jesus to be: "A light for the nations, to open the eyes of the blind, to bring prisoners from confinement and from the dungeon, those who live in darkness." The suffering servant will gladly and freely take up his destiny and vocation from the Father and fulfill it loyally.

Jesus is the coeternal, coequal Son who is God before all ages, who becomes a servant in order to reconcile humankind to the Father. His will be a terrifying, agonizing task. The psalmist's words belong to him today at this beginning of Holy Week: "Defend me, Lord, from all my foes; take up your arms and come swiftly to my aid, for you have the power to save me" (Entrance Antiphon). But the Father reassures him, and he can use the words of another psalm: "The Lord is my light and my salvation, whom should I fear" (Responsorial Psalm)?

Jesus is human, he expresses human needs, the same ones we all have. Above all, he expresses the need for friendship and love that the Creator planted in every human heart. That need is wonderfully dramatized in today's Gospel. It is just six days before the last Passover of his life. He is in the home of his friends, Martha, Mary, and Lazarus, each of whom eagerly desires to shower him with love. And each does it by doing for him what each does best. Martha cooks and serves him a meal. The evangelist doesn't tell us what Lazarus does, so we can presume that he just stands there and is available, probably somewhat distracted and puzzled after his re-entry into life after those four days in the tomb, full of gratitude to Jesus and wondering what will happen next.

Then there is Mary, doing what she does best — pouring out her love in a lavish display of generosity that will cause her to live forever in human hearts and minds. And we can't forget Judas. He provides the awful contrast. Angry, disillusioned, resentful, observing the action, he makes snide remarks and waits for he knows not what.

And finally, there is Jesus. Do we dare to try to enter into his mind at this moment? He knows he is doomed. He is aware of the hatred gathering around him in Jerusalem—hatred that will bring about a most disgraceful and terrible death for him. But we also know that he is grateful to Martha, Mary, and Lazarus for their friendship, love, and hospitality. He will allow nothing to rob him of this last beautiful moment of human love made flesh for him by his friends.

It's hard to leave this scene. It's hard even to know how to end it, especially because we, too, know what the rest of the week is going to bring. We've been speaking of human love—our need to possess it and to demonstrate it, as the Bethany family did. One thing we now know from the example of the two sisters Martha and Mary: We demonstrate our love for Christ best by doing for him what we best know how to do with the talents God himself has given to each of us in whatever vocation he has called us.

But we know, too, that human love, magnificent though it may be, is not the ultimate human fulfillment. Human love reaches its highest potential when it leads to that love for the Father which Jesus makes possible for us by his death and resurrection made present for us in Holy Week and thereafter, as often as we desire, in the Eucharist. This is the Gospel. This is the Good News of the Lord! Thanks be to God!

* * *

"A bruised reed he shall not break, and a smoldering wick he shall not quench, until he establishes justice on the earth" *(Reading I).*

"The Lord is my light and my salvation; whom should I fear" *(Responsorial Psalm).*

"Mary brought a pound of costly perfume made from genuine aromatic nard, with which she anointed Jesus' feet. Then she dried his feet with her hair" *(Gospel).*

READING I   **Isa 49:1-6**
GOSPEL   **John 13:21-33, 36-38**

Reading I: The liturgy presents another of the Servant Songs from Isaiah: "You are my servant, he said to me, Israel, through whom I show my glory."

Gospel: John describes the part of the Last Supper when Jesus announces his betrayal by Judas and the denials of Peter.

Tension is mounting in these Holy Week Masses, and it has to be more than hindsight on our part. The Gospel will make the Last Supper present for us, but already in the Entrance Antiphon we hear the psalmist declare: "False witnesses have stood up against me, and my enemies threaten violence; Lord, do not surrender me to their power!" The words now belong to Jesus. Marveling at the foresight of the prophets is never out of place for us Christians!

Reading I is another of those beautiful Servant Songs from Isaiah. The prophet may originally have had Israel herself in mind in these songs, but we see and hear Jesus himself as their fulfillment. Jesus, Servant of the Servants of God, speaks: "Hear, O coastlands, listen, O distant peoples. The Lord called me from birth, from my mother's womb he gave me my name." We know, of course, that the name chosen by the Father for his Son was *Jesus*, which means "Savior," because he is to save his people from their sins.

The prophecy now has the Father himself speaking: "You are my servant, Israel, through whom I show my glory." This means that Jesus is a "sacrament," the most splendid of all the sacraments. He can say with absolute truth: "I am made glorious in the sight of the Lord, and my God is now my strength!" The invisible, all-perfect, all-holy Lord makes himself visible in Christ Jesus our Savior and brother! This truth might well give us a fresher insight into the nature of our sacraments that we are accustomed to. These "extensions of the humanity of Christ" (St. Leo) show him to us and bring him into every aspect of our lives.

But back to the prophecy and to the last word, which again belongs to the Father: "I will make you a light to the nations, that my salvation may reach to the ends of the earth." But before he really becomes that great light, Jesus has to go through a disgraceful death. Good Friday comes before Easter Sunday.

The Jesus we see and hear in the Gospel is "deeply troubled," but he is in control. In a way, he is a kind of judge presiding over a betrayal in which he himself is to be the victim. It's not hard to imagine the anguish he feels. Judas was his man, his friend, chosen to be one of the Founding Twelve of his Church. But Judas cannot accept Jesus' ideas of the nature of his messiahship. Disillusioned, he betrays Jesus and plots to hand him over to his enemies. But Jesus does not give up on Judas without a struggle. As we shall see, even in Gethsemane, after the traitor has brought the police to arrest his master, Jesus continues to call him "Friend."

The sadness of the Last Supper is still not finished. Jesus undergoes a final wrench of pain when he foretells Peter's denials: "I tell you truly, the cock will not crow before you have three times disowned me." Betrayed, about to be disowned and forsaken by his friends, hurt to the quick, Jesus is now ready to plod to Gethsemane where, sweating blood, he will pray that the Father will remove the chalice of suffering and death from him. But he will remember the name given him from his mother's womb by the Father. He will be mindful again of his vocation, his destiny, and will cry out: "Not my will but thine be done."

* * *

"False witnesses have stood up against me, and my enemies threaten violence; Lord, do not surrender me into their power" (*Entrance Antiphon*).

"I will make you a light to the nations, that my salvation may reach to the ends of the earth" (*Reading I*).

"Hail to our king, obedient to his Father, he went to his crucifixion like a gentle lamb" (*Gospel Verse*).

READING I   Isa 50:4-9
GOSPEL   Matt 26:14-25

Reading I: Isaiah foretells grim details of the torment of the Suffering Servant: He will be beaten, his beard plucked out, and he will be spit upon.

Gospel: Matthew gives details of Judas' plot to betray Jesus, followed by the Last Supper scene in which Jesus lets Judas know that he is aware of the betrayal.

Today's Servant Song (Reading I) is a kind of meditation on the part of the Servant that might well be Jesus' own reflections on what is about to happen to him. God has given him a well-trained tongue that he might know how to speak to the weary a word that will rouse them. He has not rebelled, has not resisted the divine summons. On the contrary, he has given his back to those who beat him, his cheeks to those who plucked his beard, and he has not shielded his face from buffets and spitting.

The Responsorial Psalm also belongs to Jesus, going even more deeply into the anguish and agony. He bears insult, shame covers his face, he becomes an outcast from his brothers. Insult has broken his heart and he is weak. He looks for sympathy and comfort and finds none. Rather, his enemies put gall in his food, and for his thirst they give him vinegar to drink. But he is not overcome; out of his anguish he exclaims: "I will praise the name of God in song, and I will glorify him with thanksgiving." And all through the psalm runs the refrain that Jesus is more than willing to share with us: "Lord, in your great love, answer me."

The Gospel zeroes in on Judas again, and that can make a person wonder. Why so much prominence for this tragic character in the Gospels? Is it because Judas is a universal human figure—a person who dramatizes sin, not only his own but the sin of our first parents, the sin of everyone? Is it because there is a presence of evil in the world that needs to be recognized for what it is? Is it that there is a potential for evil in all our hearts that we need to recognize and come to terms with? These are questions each of us has to try to answer.

It is at a family meal, a love-feast, the Passover, that Jesus confronts his betrayer. At this love-feast there is a man without love. Judas knows it, Jesus knows it. Even the other disciples do not seem too sure of their fidelity. "Is it I, Lord?" they ask. It is a question that may indicate a dim awareness of the potential for evil in their own hearts. The dim awareness is going to become a reality. Except for John, they will all desert their Lord.

If the disciples are uncertain about their loyalty, Judas is not. He knows what he has deliberately planned. The disciples will sin out of weakness, Judas as a result of free, intentional plotting. His is the greater sin. But Jesus does not easily give up on him. Judas has been his friend. He chose him as a disciple, lived intimately with him for three years, shared divine secrets with him. So even now, hoping against hope, he tries to win his friend back. But Judas' heart is set. He resists grace, resists love. He has sealed his own doom.

It is hard to know what motivated Judas. It may have been disappointment at learning that Jesus was not to be a political messiah. It may have been that the love Jesus offered him was too challenging, too threatening. In any case, it was not the kind of love that Judas wanted: It implied too much responsibility on his part, so he turned it down.

Christ offers that same kind of love to us. Whether or not we accept it depends on our willingness to accept the responsibility of being loved with a divine love and doing all that we can to share that love with others. "Father, the eucharist proclaims the death of your Son. Increase our faith in its saving power and strengthen our hope in the life it promises" (Prayer After Communion). If there is anything that can prepare us for full and responsible discipleship with Jesus, it is the Eucharist.

* * *

"Jesus became obedient for us even to death, dying on the cross. Therefore, to the glory of God the Father, Jesus is Lord" (Entrance Antiphon).

"Insult has broken my heart, and I am weak, I looked for sympathy, but there was none, for comforters, and I found none" (Responsorial Psalm).

"The Son of Man did not come to be served, but to serve, and to give his life as a ransom for many" (Communion Antiphon).

READING I   Exod 12:1-14

GOSPEL   John 13:1-15

READING II   1 Cor 11:23-26

Reading I: We hear the account of the original Passover meal in all its details, along with God's command that it be observed every year as a memorial feast.

Reading II: St. Paul tells of the Lord's Supper, the first Mass.

Gospel: John describes Jesus' act of washing the feet of the disciples at the Last Supper.

Today's feast contains a wealth of themes to meditate on, such as the original Passover of the Jews, the new covenant instituted by Jesus, the priesthood, the real nature of the Eucharist, even the treason of Judas. But the Church chooses for today's Gospel John's account of Jesus washing the feet of his disciples, with special emphasis on Peter's reluctance to allow Jesus to wash his feet and Jesus' reaction to Peter's words.

According to Msgr. Romano Guardini in *The Lord* (Chicago: Henry Regnery, 1954, 361ff.), the basic idea of the entire Holy Thursday Mass is contained in the symbolic sign of the washing of the feet of the disciples by Jesus, God's own Son. This is not only the basic idea of Holy Thursday, but also it is the key to the mystery of the Eucharist and of the entire redemptive act of Christ *and* of our life as Christians.

John's description of what Jesus does — so full of drama — readily imprints itself on our minds. It is not hard to picture Jesus going from one to the other with the basin and towel, as they all sit there, bewildered, humbled, perhaps even troubled. Then he comes to Peter, who cries: "You shall never wash my feet!" And Jesus responds: "If I do not wash you, you will have no share in my heritage." Those words are the key to the meaning of the entire incident: "If *I* do not wash you . . . ." This is more than an act of humble service, although he himself tells them and us that we must imitate him in washing one another's feet. It points to the very nature of Jesus' redeeming life and work: It is not we who redeem ourselves by anything we do; it is even more than allowing ourselves to be washed; *it is Jesus proclaiming himself as the Savior,* the *only* Savior.

When it is all over, he once more takes his place at table and says to them: "If I washed your feet . . . then you must wash each other's feet. What I just did was to give you an example: as I have done, so you must do." The words are now for us. What does Christ mean? Our first reaction would probably be that he is giving us an object lesson in service, that he is preaching by personal example. But it would be a mistake to see his words and deed in that kind of moralistic light.

No, Christ's actions here flowed from the very nature of his being. The reason why Jesus in his word and action is exemplary for us is that it is in him that *our Christian life begins.* For us to imitate Christ, says Guardini, especially in this act of slavish service, means not to copy him literally, but to live in him and learn from him to do hour by hour what is right, what he would do. More exactly, it means to let him live in us so that what we do flows from his own being-in-us.

But let us look into this act of Jesus. It is an act of deepest humility. What does that mean? He who knows himself to be Lord and Master assumes the role and function of a slave. He literally empties himself in utmost humility. Strange as it might seem to us, humility is a divine quality. He who is God recognizes the mysterious dignity of these men. This is what the foot-washing means, but not all that it means.

It is not an act of self-abasement. Jesus does not degrade himself. We may recall St. Paul's words in Philippians: "Though he was in the form of God he did not deem equality with God something to be grasped at. Rather he *emptied himself* and took the form of a slave, being born in the likeness of men." Guardini insists that it is Jesus *as God* who empties himself; he "cancels his being," as it were, to assume the nature of a slave. He "abandons himself to the void, to destruction." If we do not understand how all this can be, we shall have to be content with Christ's words to Peter: "You may not realize now what I am doing, but later you will understand. . . . If I do not wash you, you will have no part in my heritage."

This seems to mean that as Christ's followers we must participate in the mystery of divine surrender, not only accept it but also participate in it. This is the core of Christianity. So the Christian life is not just imitating Christ and doing what he did. It is not just *learning* humility and mutual love from him; it is actually participating in the mystery of Christ's own surrender.

The Habit of Being is a collection of the letters of Flannery O'Connor. Her habit of being consisted in an attitude or quality, not only of action but of interior disposition. It was a habit in her inmost soul that blossomed and made her into a deeply religious, humane, generous, insightful person, who is surely one of the glories of American Catholicism. But now I see her habit of being as a sharing in Christ's own being, a sharing that he gives to us all in baptism and which he renews in every Eucharist. So, what Jesus did at the Last Supper, he enables us to do to and for one another if we are willing to come to him empty-handed and empty-hearted, aware of our utter need for him, willing to accept his gift (Rosemary Brosseau, C.N.D. Homiletic Service, Ottawa, March–April 1981, 44).

That night at the Last Supper—so present to our minds and hearts at this moment—Jesus stood at the brink of destruction. His whole system rebelled against what was to happen, but he did not hesitate. He went from that first Mass to Gethsemane, to the praetorium, to Calvary, to death, and only then to resurrection.

Every Christian one day reaches the point where she or he must be ready to accompany Jesus along that same path into destruction and death. Whatever it might be—suffering, dishonor, loss of loved ones, or the shattering of a life-long ambition—this is the decisive test of our faith. And no one will blame us if it is precisely this that we fear in Christianity. Christianity for us, our following Christ, is not adhering to a system of ethics. Being a Christian means participating, sharing in the life, in the inmost being of Jesus—his entire inmost being—for only that brings resurrection.

"He emptied himself and took the form of a slave . . . and being born in the likeness of men. He was known to be of human estate, and it was thus that he humbled himself, obediently accepting even death, death on a cross!"

This is what Jesus had in mind for us when he said: "If I washed your feet—I who am Teacher and Lord—then you must wash each other's feet."

* * *

"We should glory in the cross of our Lord Jesus Christ, for he is our salvation, our life and our resurrection; through him we are saved and made free" (Entrance Antiphon).

"How shall I make a return to the Lord for all the good he has done for me? The cup of salvation I will take up, and I will call upon the name of the Lord" (Responsorial Psalm).

"Every time you eat this bread and drink this cup, you proclaim the death of the Lord until he comes" (Reading II)!

READING I   Isa 52:13–53:12   READING II   Heb 4:14-16; 5:7-9
GOSPEL   John 18:1–19:42

Reading I: Today's Suffering Servant song tells of a lamb led to the slaughter or a sheep before the shearers. He was silent and opened not his mouth. "The Lord has laid on him the guilt of us all."

Reading II: Jesus is our supreme High Priest who knows our human condition and suffered death for our sake.

Gospel: We hear the account of the Passion of our Lord Jesus Christ according to John.

Though John's is the main Gospel of the day, we can draw on all the evangelists for details of Jesus' agony and death. We can follow him through the torment of his betrayal, his agony in the garden, the mock trial, the carrying of the cross, his being nailed to it, and hanging there in pain and utter desolation. His awful cry of abandonment still echoes through the ages: "My God, my God, why have you forsaken me?"

May we be permitted to wonder how the Father feels about that question? Why did God seem to abandon Jesus? Was the Father totally oblivious of the Passion of his Son? Maybe a hint of an answer is to be found in the writings of St. Ignatius of Antioch who once spoke about "the passion of my God." Taking off from that idea, Fr. John O'Donnell, S.J., has written that the Father was personally involved in Christ's suffering, that he actually participated in it. The Father was not an executioner, but a fellow-sufferer. More than that, O'Donnell claims that our history today is still "the largely suffering history of God. In the cross of Jesus God once and for all sided with the wretched of the earth—those beyond human hope" (*Commonweal*, April 9, 1976, 236). So the Father is not a bystander any more than we are.

The idea of the Father's personal involvement in Jesus' Passion gives at least a tiny glimpse into the mystery of human suffering that surrounds us on all sides: suffering that is man-made, like war and torture, and that which results from earthquakes, storms, tidal waves, etc. The Father continues to suffer with starving children, the maimed and crippled victims of ongoing evil that abounds in our world. Jesus is risen from the dead, says O'Donnell, and with his resurrection has dawned the sure hope of God's final victory over evil. But for us and for our world, the victory is incomplete—it is not yet a total victory. The cross of Jesus will remind us of this fact until he comes again.

So it is good and necessary for us to contemplate Jesus on the cross in all his agony. We need that vision in our lives if for no other reason than to realize how very much we are loved by Jesus. Without the cross, life is meaningless, and the world's suffering is meaningless. We need the cross to comprehend something of the immensity of evil in the world, above all, the floodtide of human evil that has been brewing in human hearts since the original Fall, the sum total of evil to which most of us have made our personal contribution.

In facing the problem and mystery of suffering, then, Christianity takes its inspiration from Jesus. He shows us how to confront suffering: He embraces it and turns it into an expression of love, of redemptive salvation for ourselves and for others. In Reading I, Isaiah puts it so beautifully:

> Ours were the sufferings he bore,
>   ours the sorrows he carried.
> But we, we thought of him as someone punished,
>   struck by God, brought low.
> Yet he was pierced for our faults,
>   crushed for our sins;
> on him lies a punishment that brings us peace,
>   and through his wounds we are healed.

We may wonder how we can best respond to the vision of God's only Son on the cross. The answer to that question may well be found in the person from whom we least expect to receive spiritual direction — the Good Thief hanging on his own cross alongside Jesus. We may see him as a universal representative person, with whom we can identify. He has lived for himself all his life. He has been a sinner. He has forsaken the God who made him. But now the presence of the innocent Jesus at his side transforms him. He sees himself for what he is, a sinner in need of a Savior. From the depths of his conversion experience, he cries out to Jesus: "Jesus, remember me when you come into your kingdom." Does he know what he is asking? "Remember me, Jesus . . . ." He couldn't have made a more perfect prayer.

Why? Because the remembering of Jesus is unlike that of any human person. It is not a mental exercise in recalling the past. When Jesus remembers, he creates and recreates, he restores, reconciles, renews, gives new life. When Jesus remembers, he shares himself — his life, his love, his glory. Reigning on the cross, Jesus even now dispenses salvation. As François Mauriac says, "A lone moment of pure love and a whole life of crime was blotted out!"

The Good Thief teaches us how to love, how to respond to love, how to make the Good Friday of Jesus our very own. "Jesus, remember us all!"

* * *

"My trust is in you, O Lord; I say, 'You are my God.' In your hands is my destiny; rescue me from the clutches of my enemies and persecutors" (*Responsorial Psalm, Reading I*).

"Christ became obedient for us even to death, dying on the cross. Therefore God raised him on high and gave him the name above all other names" (*Gospel Verse*).

"We worship you, Lord, we venerate your cross, we praise your resurrection. Through the cross you brought joy to the world" (*Antiphon for Veneration of the Cross*).

42   EASTER VIGIL

The Liturgy of the Word consists of Old Testament readings "recalling how God saved his people throughout history and, in the fullness of time, sent his own Son to be our Redeemer (Introduction to the Readings).

Reading I
(of Mass):   St. Paul presents his theology of baptism: We are baptized into the death of Christ and with him we rise again (Rom 6:3-11).

Gospel: Matthew, Mark, and Luke each relate the account of Christ's resurrection and his first appearance to the faithful women who had come to anoint his body.

Tonight we shall know that Jesus, who claimed to be the Light of the World, is indeed the Light of the World. The symbolism of the Easter candle entering the darkened church tells us vividly of the reality of Jesus, whose death we celebrated yesterday, risen now in our midst. "Light of Christ!" the priest will chant. And all will respond with joy-filled hearts, "Thanks be to God!" Our celebration of the resurrection is our personal affirmation of and our belief in the real presence of Jesus in our midst — in each of our hearts and in the heart of the living community. "Let us sing to the Lord; he has covered himself with glory!"

In Jesus all the thousands of years of humankind's longing desire and hope are fulfilled. All the great symbols, types, figures, and prophecies of the Old Testament, those marvellous teaching aids God thought up for the loving instruction of the hearts of his people — the paschal lamb, the Exodus, the wandering in the desert, the covenant on Sinai (all reviewed for us in the Liturgy of the Word tonight) — all come to fulfillment now in our midst. Christ, our Passover, has been sacrificed. But he is risen from the dead!

During the first week of Lent we prayed: "Father, through the discipline of Lent help us to grow in our desire for you." The resurrection of Christ is the ultimate answer to our prayer, to the deepest desires of our hungry hearts. "As the deer longs for the fountain of living water, so does my soul long for you, O Lord." My soul thirsts for God, for the living God. When shall I come and see the face of God" (Responsorial Psalm, Reading VII)?

I have already referred to the lovely symbolism of the Easter candle entering the darkened church and our acclaiming the risen Christ whom the candle represents. But its symbolism is inexhaustible. Soon after the Easter candle is carried into the church, the candles in our hands will burn with the new light from it. It is a perfect indication of our willingness to share in the resurrection of Jesus by continuing to die to sin and rise to a new and more fervent life of grace. But more than all else, the one light in all our hands coming from the Christ-candle tells us of *our oneness in Christ.* There is one heart beating through all the community — the heart of Jesus, the Risen Savior.

"Why do you search for the living among the dead?" the angel asks us. "He is not here, he has been raised up." And we have died and have risen with him, for tonight our personal entering into, our possessing his death and resurrection through our baptism, is going to be renewed. We were buried with Christ by our baptism into his death, and so, as Christ has risen from the dead by the glory of God the Father, we may walk in newness of life (Rom 6:4-6).

The Church never lets us forget our baptism, especially not during Lent and our Easter celebration. She constantly reminds us that baptism is not a past reality, but an ever-present experience for and in us. St. Paul tells us in Reading I that we are to walk in newness of life, and we may well wonder what this newness of life consists in. Surely, it means more than new habits of living or refraining from old ones, important as that may be. Newness of life for us *is a new principle of life* in our hearts. "If anyone is in Christ, he is a new creation," St. Paul tells us (2 Cor 5:17). "The old order has passed away; now all is new."

One of the prayers of the Easter Vigil puts it perfectly: "Almighty and eternal God, you created all things in wonderful beauty and order. Help us to perceive how still more wonderful is the new creation by which in the fullness of time you redeemed your people through the sacrifice of our passover, Jesus Christ . . . ."

Easter joy, a foretaste of the joy of heaven, begins tonight. Joy reigns supreme. But daily life and living will go on. We will still work, still suffer, still worry, and we may even sin again, returning to our old routines and prejudices. But Jesus will not give up on us. He will live with us and will make his life, death, and resurrection present to and for us as long as he lives. We may not forget that our thirsting for God and his love cannot begin to compare with the thirst he has for us and for our love. Maybe we had just better give up running away from him and allow him to catch and possess us. For only then will we truly grasp the real meaning of Easter and the resurrection of Jesus, the Lord.

* * *

"Give thanks to the Lord, for he is good, for his mercy endures forever" (Responsorial Psalm).

"I saw water flowing from the right side of the temple, alleluia. It brought God's life and his salvation, and the people sang in joyful praise: "alleluia, alleluia" (Antiphon After Renewal of Baptismal Vows).

"Christ has become our paschal sacrifice; let us feast with the un- leavened bread of sincerity and truth, alleluia" (Communion An- tiphon).